Praise for *The Miracle Mentality*

"The quality of your life is determined by the quality of your mindset! Tim Storey has been helping people transform their lives for decades and his timeless wisdom in this book will support you in turning any setback into your biggest comeback!"

—LEWIS HOWES

"You are incredibly powerful. And that's the good news and the bad news. You can make anything happen with the right thinking—and you also can make a lot of bad stuff happen to you with the wrong thinking. Mindset and how you approach life, business, and problems determines the outcome and conditions of your life. You can do anything with the right mindset."

—GRANT CARDONE

"The quality of our lives is directly correlated to the quality of our thoughts. My friend Tim Storey understands miraculous thinking better than anyone I know."

—ED MYLETT

"I have known Tim Storey for quite some time now, and his dedication to spirituality and mental health are unparalleled. *The Miracle Mentality* is just that. In his new book, Tim captures the essence of what a miracle really looks like, and it only made me believe in them more."

—DYLAN MCDERMOTT

"Mindset: pay attention to what you are paying attention to. Your mindset is *everything* when it comes to championship—champion living, champion giving, champion choices, and champion impact."

—GLORIA MAYFIELD BANKS

"The mind is where everything begins. It's the mental gatekeeper to all of your hopes and dreams and treasures. A right mind means right actions. Free your mind, and everything good will follow!"

—VERDINE WHITE

"I'm aware that there are several types of mindsets, two of them being a fixed mindset and a growth mindset. Personally, I feel like I have more of a growth mindset. I believe I have the ability to change my opinion if I learn something new, or something that might be better for me. My desire is to keep hope alive, and remain teachable to the end.

Of course, there are certain things I believe in: love, truth, compassion, forgiveness, prayer, redemption, and character. I believe in a Power greater than myself. I study to encourage and inspire myself and my behavior accordingly. Thank you, God, and thank you, Tim, for continuing to shine the light on tools to help us be better, and do better, always."

—RUTH POINTER

"I believe in miracles. I can truly say miracles have changed my life. Some miracles come right away; other miracles take time. Tim Storey's new book will teach you to step into miracle living. Depend on God, and He will bring you daily miracles."

—DUANE "DOG" CHAPMAN

"The right mindset will take you from good to great. If you can control your mind, you can control your level of success. Tim taught me to believe in miracles, and that allowed me to start receiving miracles!"

—CAYLA CRAFT

"I've known Tim for twenty-five years; he's been one of my closest friends. I've never known someone so dedicated to helping other people. Every waking moment of his life, he's on a call, Zoom, or speaking engagement. Tim has your best interests at heart—he only wants to see you succeed. I love *The Miracle Mentality*, which is exactly what all of us need at this time."

—BRENT BOLTHOUSE

"Your external world is a reflection of your internal world. Everything you see in this world is created in someone's mind. What are you creating?"

—RAJA DHALIWAL

"Having a Miracle Mentality allows you to focus on your purpose and the positive outcome you are here to create. Any adversity you may face creates the opportunity to forge your strengths along your journey. As Tim Storey shares, 'If you have a setback, don't take a step back—get ready for the comeback.' Prepare yourself for the greatest comeback, as Tim guides you on how to turn your Miracle Mentality into reality."

—SHARON LECHTER

"Mindset is everything. Every day you wake up with a choice to have positive or negative thoughts—choosing positive ones sets the tone for your entire day. Over the years, Tim has been a huge source of encouragement. He is all about positivity and believing when we have a setback, it is setting us up for an amazing comeback."

—CHRISTINA ANSTEAD

"Having the right mindset is the beginning of being successful. All of my successes in life can be attributed to having a correct mindset. Contrarily, all of my failures are directly attributed to me going into that situation with the wrong mindset. Without God in your life, it's almost impossible to have the proper mindset.

I was thankful two weeks before I met my wife, I *changed* my mindset when I decided to give my life to Christ. So a notch in my belt was no longer the mission—it was now to have a real relationship. That change of mind has led to a twenty-four-year marriage!"

—TIM BROWN

"I've known Tim Storey for many years, and he's a visionary. He's always talked about changing your mindset, winning, and seeking higher goals. He continues to speak life into me, so I know this book, *The Miracle Mentality*, will speak life into you."

—ROBERT TOWNSEND

"*The Miracle Mentality* engages us on a journey of rediscovering the importance of miracles, whether big or small. Tim's insight and personal experiences are seamlessly woven throughout the threads of this book, perfectly. If you desire to maximize your potential and see your greatness manifested, the powerful words in this book by Tim Storey will not disappoint."

—TIM TIMBERLAKE

"You have something special—you have *greatness* within *you*!

My name is Les Brown, speaker, author, trainer, and friend of Tim Storey. I am sincerely honored to recommend Tim's new blockbuster book *The Miracle Mentality.*

I believe, and I am sure that you will agree, that the launching of this powerful book, at this time when so many are in panic mode, is a God moment.

If there has ever been a time when a miracle was needed, it's now. Indeed, we are in a global and collective fight to maintain our inner peace, keep the faith, and have a spirit of optimism. This book will show you how to make an impact with your life in spite of the coronavirus, the changing political climate, and everything else that appears to be working against us.

Tim Storey—iconic speaker, coach, and mentor to many, including me—has given us a survivor's guide and the master key we all so desperately need to grow through this experience we are currently facing. He shows us that miracles happen every day and that they begin in our own minds.

The Miracle Mentality is a masterpiece of mental stamina, where every page will take you to a part of you that you can't get to by yourself. Get ready for your transformation into developing your own Miracle Mentality!"

—LES BROWN

"I believe in the power of walking with expectancy, and no one sets you up to do that better than my good friend Tim Storey. In a world that wants you to walk in fear, expect less and play small, *The Miracle Mentality* will equip with you with a mindset of limitless possibility."

—PATRICE WASHINGTON

THE
Miracle
MENTALITY

THE
Miracle
MENTALITY

Tap into the Source of Magical
Transformation in Your Life

TIM STOREY

with Nick Chiles

HARPER HORIZON

Published by Harper Horizon, an imprint of HarperCollins Focus LLC.

Any internet addresses, phone numbers, or company or product information printed in this book are offered as a resource and are not intended in any way to be or to imply an endorsement by Harper Horizon, nor does Harper Horizon vouch for the existence, content, or services of these sites, phone numbers, companies, or products beyond the life of this book.

Unless otherwise indicated, Scriptures are taken from the King James Version of the Bible. Public domain.

Scripture quotations marked NIV are taken from the Holy Bible, New International Version®, NIV®. Copyright © 1973, 1978, 1984, 2011 by Biblica, Inc.™ Used by permission of Zondervan. All rights reserved worldwide. www. zondervan.com. The "NIV" and "New International Version" are trademarks registered in the United States Patent and Trademark Office by Biblica, Inc.™

ISBN 978-0-7852-3673-3 (eBook)
ISBN 978-0-7852-3672-6 (HC)

Library of Congress Cataloging-in-Publication Data

Library of Congress Control Number: 2020944775

Printed in the United States of America
21 22 23   LSC   10 9 8 7 6 5 4 3 2 1

Contents

CHAPTER 1

Discovering the Miracle Mentality

I was seven years old the first time I visited Disneyland in California with my family. And boy, was my mind blown. As I walked around the park and experienced the rides, everything I saw amazed me. *How is this possible?* I asked myself. The rockets in Tomorrowland. The roller coaster shooting through the Matterhorn. The incredibly lifelike robotic bears in the Country Bear Jamboree. All the people from around the globe at It's a Small World. One word kept coming back to me: *magical*. Everything at Disneyland felt like magic, existing outside the boundaries of what I had come to know as the real world.

Disneyland has cultivated this reaction since its opening in 1955—moving visitors, especially young children, to marvel at the possibility of miracles. I think often about that first visit to

1

Disneyland because it highlights how at a young age we're conditioned to believe in the power of miracles. In other words, most of us begin our lives imbued with a Miracle Mentality. But over the years, things happen that cause it to slip away. Disappointment. Disaffection. Pain. Loss. Depression.

My purpose in this book is to help you figure out how to reconnect with the Miracle Mentality that buoyed you in childhood, that made you an infectious carrier of joy. What did you believe would happen in the early morning hours of December 25? That a fat dude in a red suit would slide down your chimney and bring you a bounty of toys. That belief is nothing but the Miracle Mentality in overdrive. How about when you lost a tooth and gleefully slid it underneath your pillow before you went to sleep? The expectation that some kind of glittery tooth fairy would slip into your bedroom and replace the tooth with cold, hard cash is as miraculous as the guy in the red suit.

Childhood is an endless case study in the power of the Miracle Mentality.

A year after that first Disneyland visit, a group of missionaries visited our church, the First Family Church of Los Angeles. The missionaries regaled the congregation with stories of their visits to foreign lands, where they said they were using the power of God to heal people by praying for them. I sat up in my pew, immediately drawn to this talk of the supernatural. *God has the power to perform miracles?* I hadn't heard this before. And I was hooked.

The next year the church invited a pastor from Sri Lanka to preach. At first I was captivated because I'd never heard of Sri Lanka and thought it was a cool-sounding name. But what happened next astonished me. This pastor announced he was going to heal people in my church, using the power of prayer. People walked up to the front in droves—church members with arthritis, migraines, and breathing problems. They lined up—and then proclaimed they were healed of their ailments after he prayed for them and laid his hands on them. The church was abuzz with the miracles taking place. When folks were healed, they'd get deeply emotional. Their wails and sobs bounced off the church walls and ceilings, creating a dramatic spectacle unlike anything I'd ever seen.

I don't remember every detail, but my mother told me I got up from my pew—we usually sat in the fifth row—and walked to the front of the church, where I stood next to the line of about a dozen people waiting to be healed. Apparently, my amazement was evident because our pastor said, "Oh, little Timmy Storey finds this fascinating!" The congregation laughed.

I was mesmerized—the stuff the missionary had told us about was happening right here, in front of my face, to people I'd known most of my life. Every person who walked out of the church that day, including me, was filled with the Miracle Mentality.

To believe in miracles, to be open to the idea that wonderful things can sweep into your life, you don't necessarily need to witness a scene like the one I saw in church that day. You can look at your own life and the lives of people you know. If we start to probe, I'm sure we can find evidence of the miraculous. I believe each of us has been anointed. I'm a Christian, so I use the word *God* to describe the Almighty, but all of the world's major religions speak of the healing power of the supernatural. The Quran speaks in many places about the power of *shifa*, miraculous cures that Allah brings to those who have real belief in their hearts. The Torah discusses how miracles are evidence of the omnipotence of God. Buddhists profess that Buddha revealed his miraculous powers from the moment of his birth, when he took seven steps and proclaimed he was chief of the world. I've brought healing to people from every religion you can imagine—Buddhists, Muslims, shamans.

I believe the Miracle Mentality is innate. We are made in the image of God and—to quote Kendrick Lamar—we have royalty in our DNA. Through *education, observation*, and *conversation*, we all can draw out what's already there. Unfortunately, many of us experience a lack of education, or a subpar education, and a scarcity of observation, and the wrong conversation. Subsequently, our Miracle Mentality is suppressed. For many of us, that's called "life." But if you put someone in the proper environment, if you work to change their perspective on the world—adding the right kinds of education, observation, and conversation—you can change everything. They'll "discover" the power of the Miracle Mentality.

And you might be pleased to hear it's never too late to bring about the change.

Maybe it's because I'm from Southern California, but I've always been a big movie buff. In the movie *The Shawshank Redemption*, adapted from a Stephen King short story, Morgan Freeman's character is a wonderfully dramatic illustration of the Miracle Mentality. Despite everything he's been through, he retains his sense of wonderment and awe. He knows something better for him is out there.

In the more recent film *Just Mercy*, based on attorney Bryan Stevenson's book of the same name about his work trying to get innocent men off death row in the South, the death row inmate played by Jamie Foxx, Walter McMillian, is initially skeptical when he meets attorney Stevenson, played by Michael B. Jordan. McMillian was so disgracefully railroaded, he was placed on death row in 1987, before he even had a sham of a trial. He had many reasons for his skepticism after what happened to him, getting accused of killing a white woman, even though he was at a church fish fry with a large gathering of family and friends when the murder occurred. But over time, McMillian begins to trust Stevenson and eventually allows himself to believe that something good might happen to him. He starts to be overtaken with the Miracle Mentality. He starts to have hope. His hope is rewarded when his case is dismissed, and he's reunited with his family.

As demonstrated in Walter McMillian's case, many times we're led to a Miracle Mentality because we're experiencing pain. The Miracle Mentality transports us into something I call the "uncommon life"—a life lived outside of the ordinary, in an unusual manner. To get to an uncommon life, you must have uncommon dreams, which require uncommon patience. Unfortunately, many of us aren't able to summon these uncommon states until we're going through something extraordinarily difficult and trying.

I have an example from my life of having the Miracle Mentality come to me through pain after my father died in a motorcycle accident when I was eleven. As he rode his motorcycle through my hometown of Whittier, California, a police cruiser ran through a red light and crashed into him, killing him. His death consumed my entire family and locked us into agony and depression for years. In many ways, my family never recovered.

Not long after his death, one day I walked past my parents' bedroom and heard my mother sobbing behind the closed door. The agony of hearing her tears hit me in the gut. I had a choice in that moment: either get devoured by the climate now swirling around me or allow my imagination to take me outside the four walls of that small house. I chose the latter, which probably doesn't surprise you. What did I do to escape my surroundings? I watched cartoons. I found that animation helped. I also was helped by watching *Soul Train*, because I saw people having fun. In addition, listening to Motown music comforted me. I also found an escape in books. In all these ways I held on to my belief that miracles can happen.

It's one thing to capture the Miracle Mentality when you're young; it's another thing entirely to hold on to it as you grow older and are buffeted by life experiences. Most people get derailed on the way to becoming a grown-up and lose all sense of the miraculous. That's why I say that the *uncommon dream* requires *uncommon focus* and *uncommon faith*.

I visited Disneyland again a few years later, and I could see that paint on the figures in It's a Small World was cracking a bit. But I still thought the whole experience was magical, and it gave me an unparalleled feeling of elation. I had held on to my faith in the Miracle Mentality.

It's fascinating to note how age and experience attempt to eat away at your faith. For instance, maybe one day a cousin will ridicule your belief in Santa: "Don't you know it's just your dad putting out your toys?" Some other kid might tell you you're an idiot or a "baby" for believing that some glittery fairy comes into your room at night to swap your tooth for money. Other people try to chip away at your faith, at your belief in magic. They attempt to steal your innocence.

Recently I was talking to my nephew's four-year-old son and delighting in his unshakable faith in miracles.

"John, where is Santa Claus from?" I asked.

"The North Pole," he said.

"How does he get around?"

"Reindeers."

"Who's one of his main reindeers?"

"Rudolph."

"What kind of nose does he have?"

"Red," John said.

"John, how do you know all this?"

"I saw the movie."

I cracked up. He might have seen the story on television, but that didn't shake his belief that this world really existed.

I think two of the biggest things that happen to erode our faith are disappointment and disillusionment. Maybe Santa Claus didn't bring you what you asked for, so you start losing faith in him. Things aren't going your way as much, and you stop believing in the magic. Maybe you visit Disneyland and the Matterhorn is shut down. *Hey, the Matterhorn is always supposed to be there for me!*

Children come to us with a belief not only in the magical but also in the power of love. They seem instinctively to want to help other people, to show empathy and concern. And then one day they get introduced to the dark side.

That's what happened to me in the third grade. Eight-year-old Timmy Storey was in line for the water fountain with a bunch of classmates. A girl was drinking from the fountain, and she was a bit chubby. A rather large fifth grader stood behind her, waiting his turn.

"Hey, fatty!" the fifth grader said. "Hurry up, already. You're going to drink up all the water!"

Though she had to be somewhat upset, the girl turned around and said politely, "I'm almost done." She turned back to the water and kept drinking. What the fifth grader did next shocked me to my core. He reached out and slapped the back of her head. Hard.

I tapped him on the shoulder.

"Hey!" I said. "Hey, you can't do that!"

In a flash he pivoted around and grabbed me by my bushy afro. I didn't see his assault coming at all. He yanked me down and kneed me in the stomach. I buckled over. Several fifth graders quickly intervened and pushed the bully against the wall.

At the time I was already becoming known in the elementary school because of my athletic prowess. The other kids talked about how fast I was. They liked me and respected me. I was pleased so many kids came to my defense.

I didn't come away from the incident with any kind of agenda to get revenge on the bully. My reaction was astonishment that someone could be as cruel as this kid. I hadn't encountered that before. *Wow, people are mean like that, for no reason?* I thought. Up to that point I had retained a Miracle Mentality about human nature, believing everybody was as good and kind as I felt I was.

That experience taught me another lesson about the Miracle Mentality: having it will create uncommon adversaries. I'm fairly certain that bully was jealous of me. I was liked because of how far I could throw a football and how well I could catch a baseball. Those were the sorts of things that got boys respect in Whittier in the 1960s and 1970s. That probably didn't change much over the next half century.

An older kid in my neighborhood, David Gonzalez, started taking an interest in me when I was six. He was thirteen, and I'm not sure what he saw in me, but he became my personal coach in sports. He taught me how to dribble a basketball and to follow through on my jump shot until I was deadly accurate. When I had the chance to display my talents in school, I gained a whole bunch of admirers— but I also gained adversaries. The bully saw an opportunity to bring me down a few notches. However, it backfired because he found out I had a lot more allies than he did, even among the fifth graders. When you have the glow of the Miracle Mentality, it can be deeply threatening to many people.

Over the years I've discovered I have a gift, an ability to use my faith to act as a vessel, to bring the healing power of God to people in need. With the overwhelming problems most of us have to battle to stay afloat in this challenging world, I've learned that sometimes we need something uncommon working on our behalf. That's where my belief in the supernatural comes in—my belief in miracles. At times you need to call on supernatural, extraordinary powers to overcome addiction or career disaster or serious health problems.

When I tune my satellite dish to the higher power, I receive supernatural signals. I call it "tapping into the source." The Bible says that Jesus saw people hurting, and he was moved with compassion. I believe compassion is the key to my miracle work. I care so deeply for people, I am so awash with a fervent desire to help them, that I am able to draw on my strengths to bring about dramatic change in their lives.

Over the last four decades, I've discovered another powerful truth: we all have the ability to draw on miracles to bring about the change we need in our lives. I don't think I'm special in this way; I've just learned how to receive and interpret the supernatural signals I get from on high. I did this for the first time when I was in college, using the power of God to heal my roommate's ailing back. I've been doing it ever since. I am a living embodiment of the wonder of the Miracle Mentality.

Throughout my life I've been thrilled to come into contact with people who have the glow of the Miracle Mentality. Their love and their faith are infectious. Through my renown I've had the opportunity to travel around the world and minister to people in many different places. At this point I have been to 75 different countries—a sizeable percentage of the 195 countries that currently exist. What I found particularly fascinating was that many people I ministered to in these places weren't Christian.

I admit, at first I found this disconcerting. After all, I'd spent many years looking at the concept of miracles through a Christian lens, studying the many places in the Bible where Jesus performed miracles through the power of God—his power. But I'd be in Indonesia, spending all my time with Buddhists, performing miracles and hearing them talk about how they were accessing a higher power through their faith. Or I'd be on an airplane, connecting with someone who is a Muslim and hearing them describe how miracles had transformed their life. I realized that, like me, all of these people had a Miracle Mentality. They used a different path to connect with the power of God, but we were all being transformed by a higher power.

In the Christian system, we believe we're made in God's image; therefore, many of his characteristics and attributes are within us. He is a God of miracles, so he created his children and imbued them with a Miracle Mentality. There are different ways to activate these miracles. For me, I use the teachings of Christ. I spend many hours poring over the Scriptures, reading the Gospels of Matthew, Mark, Luke, and John and closely following all the places and ways Jesus performed miracles. But I've been stunned by the convergence of so many different belief systems around this idea of a Miracle Mentality.

When I'm on the road, communing with wonderful people in far-flung corners of the globe, I sometimes think about the inspirational work of the late Anthony Bourdain and I find many similarities between us. If I may stretch an analogy, I'm kind of an Anthony Bourdain for the soul. Bourdain traveled the world, discovering, conversing, meeting people, and sharing mind-blowing experiences, all centered around food. Food was the glue that held it all together, the thread that weaved through every narrative. I go around the world meeting and conversing with many different kinds of people, but my travels are all centered around spirituality, around healing and the betterment of people's lives. The foundation of my work, the methodology that nurtured me, is what I call the "Jesus Style." In Acts 10:38, the Bible says, "God anointed Jesus of Nazareth with the Holy Ghost and with power: who went about doing good, and healing all that were oppressed of the devil; for God was with him."

And in Isaiah 61:3, in a verse I have grown to love, the Bible says the Spirit of the Lord has been sent "to appoint unto them that mourn in Zion, to give unto them beauty for ashes, the oil of joy for mourning, the garment of praise for the spirit of heaviness; that they might be called trees of righteousness, the planting of the LORD, that he might be glorified." I love the message in this Isaiah verse, that the Lord went around saying that in those areas where you felt dead, he will take your dead ashes and exchange them for beauty. He doesn't say he will put beauty on top of your ashes—he will *replace* them with beauty. Jesus moved in the world spending time with a wide range of people—tax collectors, fishermen, ex-prostitutes. People very different from him, people who don't appear to be anointed.

I'm certainly not comparing my life to that of Christ, but I've found solace in the knowledge that my travels have also brought me into the space of people whose spiritual yearnings and thoughts may appear to be very different from my own. I have allowed myself to be open to spending time with people who may have different ways of talking to God and different names for him. But always they are receptive to my healing. And the healing can take many forms: sometimes it's healing through words; sometimes it's healing by bringing some sort of material aid, whether it's motivational CDs or books; sometimes it's healing by bringing a team of doctors or dentists to a certain area that hasn't had access to such healers; sometimes it's healing through supernatural means, laying on hands or helping someone figure out how to shift their satellite dish to hear God.

I've prayed with people who weren't Christian and been moved by the experience, as were they. They might not have shared the same faith, but they did share the Miracle Mentality. Based on a mentality that made them open to the power of a miracle-working God, they were able to get help for their ailments.

I used to enjoy watching when Bourdain would spend time in a corner of the world about which I was ignorant, and he'd open himself up to the sometimes outrageous-looking foods they'd serve him. When someone handed him a plate of barbecued crickets, he'd open wide and let one slide down his throat because he knew it was considered an acceptable food in that place. Crickets may not have been part of Bourdain's normal diet, but when he was with these people, he trusted them enough to open himself up to their palate. The fact that he was willing to experiment didn't mean his palate had changed. He was still going to sit down to a plate of bacon and eggs when he returned to America. But he respected the people he visited enough that he was willing to try on their palates, to step into their thinking about acceptable foods, if only for a day or two.

A few years back I had a memorable experience in this realm, courtesy of Oprah Winfrey. In addition to her many gifts, Oprah has an insatiable curiosity, which is part of what drives her to create magnetic television programming. One such example is the incredible series she did called *Belief*, which explored the nature of spirituality across the world and why people are drawn to religion and faith in a high power in so many fascinating forms. I was invited to a private screening she held in Santa Barbara, where she gathered spiritual and thought leaders from all over the world. It was a breathtaking sight—an inspiring collection of pilgrims wearing the dress of religions from across the globe. I was moved by the peaceful, harmonious vibe, all of us awash in the intensity of our love and respect for each other. After we left the movie theater, we boarded buses to travel up to Oprah's estate. I sat next to a Muslim lady, and we quickly struck up a conversation about our devotion to God.

"How long have you been close to God?" I asked her.

"Since I was a little girl," she said.

"Do you feel his presence?" I asked.

"Yes."

"How often do you pray?"

"Five times a day."

"Do you feel his presence when you pray?"

"Yes," she said.

"How does his presence feel to you?"

She thought for a moment. "Sometimes I feel it like a warmth; sometimes I feel it like an embrace, like a hug."

I was blown away because her experience was so close to mine, yet we held entirely different belief systems. At Oprah's house, when we were seated for dinner, on one side I was flanked by a Hindu woman who was a college professor and on the other side by best-selling author Gary Zukav, who wrote the influential book *The Seat of the Soul*. We dialogued about the first time we felt close to God, what prompted that moment, what the experience felt like. The sensations we described were similar to each other's, and to the Muslim woman's on the bus.

This remarkable evening strengthened my conviction and belief. Here we were, vastly different people with very different religions, from very different places, yet we were all describing similar experiences. It was a testament to the existence of the Miracle Mentality and the power of spirituality. We had all taken different paths, but we had arrived at the same place.

I have found that miraculous transformations can come at the most unexpected times. Recently I was in a taxicab in Arizona after being picked up from the airport, heading to my hotel before I was to speak at a large church. I noticed that the taxi driver kept looking at me in the rearview mirror.

"Why do I know your face?" he asked.

I shrugged. "Well, I'm on TV sometimes."

"You look very familiar. Why are you on TV?"

"Because I help people. I'm a spiritual leader. Kind of a therapist."

"A therapist? Wow! Maybe you can help me with this situation."

He told me he had fought for Iran in the Iran-Iraq War over the course of four years. He said he saw everyone around him die, including many of his friends. Ever since the war ended, he'd been so disturbed, so traumatized by what he saw, that he'd been unable to sleep. He said he never got more than three hours of sleep a night. He'd been under the care of a psychiatrist and took prescribed drugs, but he said the drugs weren't working.

"Do you believe in God?" I asked.

He was Muslim; he said that he did.

"Okay, here's what's going to happen. I have a gift," I told him. "I move in miracles. I will touch your back and you will feel power go through you. Not only will he heal your mind with all these thoughts you have, but your entire body is going to heal because you have problems with your breathing."

He gasped. "How can you know this?!"

"I told you, I have a gift in miracles." I leaned forward and saw we were approaching my hotel. "Don't pull into my hotel. Pull onto the side of the street or a parking lot."

He turned and parked across the street from the hotel.

"Close your eyes and say these words: 'Dear God, I believe that you're miraculous. I will receive my miracle right now.'" When I touched him, the power of God shot right through him.

"Oh my gosh, I feel a jolt of energy!" he shouted.

"Keep your eyes closed. That's God you're feeling."

I had him get out of the car.

"Move your neck. Move your back," I told him. He started walking back and forth on the sidewalk and sobbing as he obeyed my commands.

"Oh my God, you have the gift!" he said, hugging me tightly.

"You're gonna sleep at night; you're gonna be okay," I said. "Now go home and tell your wife what happened. Go tell her you will be a better help to her."

He looked at me in amazement and started crying even more. "How do you know these things?"

I began to be filled with a clear vision about this man. I could see it all, like a script had been laid before me. "There's something going on between you and your wife where she doesn't feel like you're there for her."

He shook his head. "There's no way anyone can know this!"

"I'm tapping into God," I told him. "Go home and tell your wife you will be a better help to her with the kids."

He covered his face and sobbed. I gave him my website address and told him he needed to start following me, to find out more about my message. After he drove across the street and I got out of the car, he hugged me again without saying another word.

That's been the story of my life for many years.

Not long ago I was speaking at a church near Baltimore, signing copies of my book *Utmost Living* in the church lobby. A little boy, no more than five, marched up to me, pointed, and said, "Mom, there he is—the miracle man!"

I smiled at him, but I was curious. "Why do you call me the miracle man?"

"You're the one doing miracles!"

He was so excited. I was tempted to go into an explanation of my process, that God was performing the miracles—I was just the vessel, the conduit.

"He loved the service!" his mother said as she walked up behind him. "He kept asking questions as he saw people getting healed."

I thought about all the kids I see at my services who are transfixed when the healing begins. And I thought back to my own reaction as a boy in my Los Angeles church. Who knows? Perhaps this boy was being drawn to his destiny, just like I was back then.

"Are you the miracle man?" he asked me once again.

I looked down at him and smiled.

"Yes. I am."

CHAPTER 2

Toiling in the Mundane, the Messy, and the Mad

In my travels I've determined that each of us lives in one of three states:

- mundane,
- messy, or
- mad.

But we all want to live in the *magical*.

Magic moments aren't preplanned. Instead, they're like divine gifts, miracles that deeply change us, bless us, and transform us. Living in the magical state imbues our life with the Miracle Mentality.

The Miracle Mentality is the state of mind, the principles, the strategy, the rules of living that set the conditions for magic to happen. It is a way to construct our lives that will lead to deeper meaning, bigger adventures, and more opportunities.

My goal with this book is to help you move from the first three states into the magical state so that you can create the conditions for miracles and transformation to enter your life.

For example, church services are designed for worshippers to have a divine experience with God. The goal of the minister is to set the conditions for that experience. Through the sharing of Scripture, worship, and prayer, everything is designed to create an atmosphere where individual worshippers can have a spontaneous spiritual experience that impacts them positively and meaningfully.

In relationships, effort is required to maintain connection and intimacy. A common piece of advice many couples' therapists give to their clients is for the couple to go on a date once a week. Spending that time together on a regular basis will go a long way to keeping the romance in a relationship alive. Why? The ritual of making a reservation, dressing up, going to a nice restaurant, giving compliments, and showing affection all set the conditions for romance to happen.

Both of these examples make the same point: if you want something special to happen, you begin by setting the conditions for it to happen. Setting those conditions creates a space, an opportunity, a moment where something meaningful can take place.

Mundane

What is the mundane? The dictionary defines *mundane* as boring, dull, monotonous, uneventful, lacking interest or excitement. I define the mundane as the known things in your life, the comfortable, the regular.

I have a relative who is known in the family for having his "spots" to eat. Whenever we go out, he always runs down the same list of the few restaurants. No matter what anyone says, he only wants to eat at the places where he knows the menu. One day, as the family was deciding where to go, someone recommended that we try a new place. My family member immediately responded negatively and was highly skeptical. He had never heard of this place before, so of course it could not be good. After a brief conversation, he was outvoted, and off we went on a new adventure to try a restaurant none of us had eaten at before. For the entire meal he was negative and critical. He could not handle being in a place that was out of his comfort zone. He was suffering from what I call "comfortable couch syndrome."

On its own, the mundane is neither positive nor negative. It's the neutral parts of life, the known quantities, the familiar, the comfortable, the everyday. But if you're not careful, you will spend too much time in the mundane and not enough time challenging yourself, learning new things, and taking on new adventures. When we spend too much time in the mundane, we begin to settle and cement ourselves where we are.

The mundane becomes negative when it becomes limiting. The mundane becomes limiting when it becomes the excuse not to grow, not to shoot for the magic, not to look for the miracle. When you only live in the comfortable, you begin to live life by default, not design. You don't take action or expand your potential and opportunities, which are the places where the magic happens.

In an episode of *Comedians in Cars Getting Coffee*, Jerry Seinfeld interviewed Sebastian Maniscalco on the best way to write comedy bits. Sebastian explained to Jerry that even though he is now rich and famous, he still does the mundane chores around the house. He still buys his own groceries and runs his own errands, even though he can now afford to hire people to do those things for him. He said being responsible for his own chores keeps him grounded and creates comedy that relates to the everyday lives of his audience. He is using the mundane to move toward the magical.

Mastering the mundane in your life (keeping your room clean, paying your bills on time, grocery shopping) keeps you committed to the responsibility of taking care of your space, of yourself, and of your property, creating an opportunity to build something on top of those actions—an opportunity to develop a Miracle Mentality. To quote Navy SEAL captain Jocko Willink, "Discipline equals freedom." Mastery of the mundane, of the regular, of the everyday habits that structure your life will mean having a strategic edge to have more freedom to enjoy life.

But too often in the mundane we are plodding along, trudging forward, pushing ourselves to get out of bed every morning and make it through another day. Many of us remain stuck in this state our entire lives. To move forward and keep the mundane from trapping us, we need to start by taking one of these three steps: *education*, *conversation*, or *observation*.

People often don't even know their lives are mundane until they come across something that removes the blinders and allows them to really see the world around them. The blinders usually come off when we become educated about things we never knew, or we have a conversation or make an observation that pushes us to see our lives in a different way. It's like when I went to Disneyland for the first time and had my mind blown.

We can become programmed during our childhood to live in the mundane when our parents push us away from magical thinking by forcing us to keep running straight ahead, even if we are running in the wrong direction, such as away from our passion for art or music, which then sets us up, as adults, to do the same. Many of us are caught in mundane jobs or in mundane relationships, but we aren't aware of it until we come across another type of workplace where we would really thrive or we discover we haven't been married to a person with whom we are ideally matched.

Mess

What is the mess? The dictionary defines *mess* as the dirty or untidy state of things or of a place. I define the messy as the undone things of life. The things that are unkept, unmanaged, unmaintained.

When someone is suffering from depression or anxiety, one of the first things a psychologist will do is take inventory of the patient's habits and life. They will ask questions like, "Are you sleeping? Do you have healthy relationships? Are you eating regularly and at proper times? Do you go to work? Have a regular schedule?" The therapist will also ask about the problem causing the depression and anxiety. Often a lack of order and problems go together. The reason: order manages the mess. The more order a person has, the smaller the mess in his or her life. If a patient has a big mess, somewhere the structures of routine, discipline, and order have broken down.

There is a concept in science called entropy, which says that all matter in the universe tends toward disorder. Translation: when things are left unchecked or unmaintained, they get messy fast. That's why we require constant care, good habits, and a desire to maintain order.

Madness

What is the madness? Madness is the behavior that breeds negative results, uncontrollable emotions, or worse behaviors. The things we do over and over that doom us to repeat our cycles of failure. The madness can affect our relationships, our children, our health, our dreams, and our aspirations. When we are steeped in drama, we have a difficult time holding it together and are often overcome by depression and extreme anxiety—states that can prompt us to reach for drugs or alcohol to escape.

I grew up with a lot of madness and mayhem. We were a family without resources. My father had a tenth-grade education; my mother, a sixth-grade education. They had never been taught strategies to handle conflict, how to properly pay their taxes, or ways to keep the household in order. Another word for what happened in my house is *drama*. And if there was no drama, my mother would create it. Drama takes away your opportunities to go into that magical, miraculous side of yourself. You're tied down, entangled in chaos and drained of your energy.

Becoming Magical

We have the power to push ourselves out of our mundane existence and to escape from the messy and the madness to get to a place where we are immersed in magical moments. When we do so, we have stepped into the Miracle Mentality. All of us have the Miracle Mentality in our DNA, but we often have difficulty recognizing it and responding accordingly.

It's interesting to watch children go through their days. We are born with magical thinking, and it's something we seek throughout our childhood. We pretend we are Superman and Wonder Woman because we recognize in them a power to make miracles happen. Usually the adults around us are the ones who drain the Miracle Mentality out of our system. In the popular TV show *Dennis the Menace*, which was big in the early 1960s (based on a comic strip), Dennis was constantly getting into trouble because of his fantastic imagination and his creativity. Most of the plot lines featured his neighbor, Mr. Wilson, trying to force the boy away from his magical thinking. But boys like Dennis grow up to be Mark Zuckerberg, Steve Jobs, and Bill Gates—people who think outside the box, who are immersed in a Miracle Mentality, never limiting what they think is possible.

A scary but powerful aspect of living in the mundane, the messy, the madness, and the magical is that in those states we establish patterns and pathways we tend to follow. Those patterns are observed and absorbed by everyone around us, including our children, and therefore we can pass these states down to our children. If we live most of our days in chaos, that's what our children begin to see as normal—and they will live their lives the same way. But if we are often in a magical state, our children grow up seeing the beauty and wonder of magical thinking. They grow into adults who live with a Miracle Mentality.

I love to watch people's reactions when I introduce these concepts to them. Their faces illuminate; they begin to see and understand where they are in their lives. I'm sure you did the same thing as you were reading the above paragraphs, taking in the descriptions and wondering in which state you are sitting right now. Throughout this book, I will teach you how to determine which states the many aspects of your life are in—and how to move into the magical state, where you will be open to the blessing of miracles in your life. I want to show you how to reach and retain the Miracle Mentality.

I give a lot of speeches and sermons across the United States and abroad. I also work with a cross section of individuals as their life coach. In other words, I regularly interact with a broad swath of humanity. I see and hear about the many problems with which humans find themselves grappling. But no matter where I go and to whom I talk, the four life states—mundane, messy, mad, and magical—always seem to resonate with people.

One of my clients with whom I do a lot of work is Paul Mitchell, the cosmetology company with more than a hundred schools across the United States. I regularly give motivational speeches to Paul Mitchell students in different cities, trying to inspire them to live magical lives. On a recent tour of schools in the heartland, in Indiana, Ohio, and Kentucky, I had a chance to learn a great deal about the young students, mostly women, who were enrolled. When I went through each of the four life states with the students in Indiana, giving examples for each one, many hands shot in the air after I paused and asked for their reactions.

One beautiful young lady said her parents got divorced when she was young, and her mother had man after man running through their house. "It was complete madness," she said. "The thought of anything magical never even went through my mind. I was just try-ing to survive and make sure nothing bad happened to me."

Another girl said that when she was growing up, her father had a problem with drugs and he was constantly fighting with her mother. "It was chaos," she said. "I think I lived between mess and madness at all times. If I ever experienced something magical, I know for sure I don't remember it. And I guarantee you I wouldn't have enjoyed it."

"Why do you say you wouldn't have enjoyed it?" I asked.

"Because I knew what mess and madness I'd have to go back to at the house."

Many in the room nodded. We were getting into it now, peeling away the facades that many of the young ladies hid behind every day.

"Wow, this magical living you talk about sounds like a fantasy I want to chase just so I have a reason to live," a young lady in Louisville said.

"What do you mean by that?" I asked.

"Well, you know, you see things on TV and you see people living amazing lives."

"Like who?" I asked.

"Like Beyoncé. Her life looks so magical. And my life is so nonmagical."

"We call it mundane," I said. "Ordinary, regular, status quo."

"Yeah, my life's mundane. I have two kids," she said.

"Are you married?"

"Yes."

"Will you let me go there with you for a minute?" I asked.

She nodded her head.

"Would you say you're happy in your marriage?"

"No."

"But you're probably going to stay—or not stay?" Then I thought about it and added, "But you don't have to answer."

"No, I want to answer. I'm going to stay. For the sake of the kids."

"How old are you?"

She told me she was twenty-four. At such a young age, she had already resigned herself to staying stuck in the mundane, maybe for the rest of her life. And rather than reaching for magic herself, she was watching other people live magical lives from afar, using their lives almost like entertainment.

"Let me follow that up for a minute," I said. "I want to understand this more. Does it seem like mundane, mess, and madness are steps you almost have to somehow get through to get to the magical?"

25

Most of the class nodded.

"So it seems like you can't skip them?"

A sharp young lady said, "Well, of course, the dream is always to skip them."

"Okay, so how does somebody skip them?"

She looked at me and smiled dreamily. "By becoming famous," she said. "By being discovered."

There it was, the new American Dream: to be famous. She had handed me one of my themes, perfectly gift wrapped. The intoxicating but destructive facade of fame seems to beckon every young person (and many not-so-young) in America. When I was in Toledo, all the students told me their town was the epitome of boring and mundane. In their minds, the only way to escape a mundane existence was to get famous and flee. Fame has become a replacement, a surrogate, for magical.

It's fascinating to me because my generation didn't have the same relationship with fame when we were younger. We were entertained by famous and talented people on television and on the athletic fields, but their lives seemed far away, not something we yearned to have ourselves. Fame wasn't the thing; the thing was the activity or the sport these people used to get their fame. If I dreamed about the life of Walt Frazier or Wilt Chamberlain or Sidney Poitier, the dream centered around becoming a fabulously talented athlete or actor, not the fame itself. You figured that if you could do the things they could do, you could live the life they lived, which you assumed was magical. But many kids today just want the fame for fame's sake, and they give little consideration to what they would do to get it.

I was having dinner recently with the writer and director Peter Landesman, who is probably best known for the Will Smith film *Concussion* about head trauma suffered by football players. Peter shared an interesting observation, one I immediately told him I would steal from him. He said fame is very much like a hologram.

We all saw the hologram of Tupac performing at the Coachella festival in 2012 and were blown away by how eerily real it felt. But we knew it wasn't really Tupac—if you reached out and tried to grab him, you would come up with air. They have holograms now that can talk back to you and interact with you as if you are speaking with an actual human—but it's still not real. According to Landesman, that's what fame is like—an illusion you can't touch or embrace. It doesn't offer a shoulder to lean on in times of need. It doesn't give you a hug when you're hurting. It can't tenderly caress your face to show you love and affection. It's a mirage. (Thanks, Peter!)

But my oh my, how that mirage has taken our society hostage. We can't escape our obsession with celebrity, even if we hid in a cave. *Access Hollywood* or *Keeping Up with the Kardashians* would certainly find us even there. Feeding the American fascination with fame has become a multibillion-dollar industry. A vast illusion is at the center of it all, propping up the entire enterprise: the idea that fame and wealth bring happiness. Bring magic. If only we could be like the celebrities we obsess over, we would be happy. And if we can't be like our favorite stars, we want to find out everything we can about them, or reach out and touch them, or even look like them. If I get injections in my butt and my lips and look like my favorite Hollywood actress, maybe I'll be as happy as I think she must be.

It didn't take long during my Paul Mitchell sessions for reality TV stars to come up.

"Look at what the Kardashians did!" one young lady said, trying to make the case that fame and fortune were the path to the magical.

"Okay, what did they do?" I asked.

"They got rich!"

The class laughed.

"But walk me through that. Like, how did they get rich?" I asked.

She said, "Well, they got a show, and now they have cosmetics."

I was waiting for her to tell me how the family's riches really began, but it soon dawned on me that none of them knew. Interestingly, their idea of fame and fortune wasn't attached to any sort of work or career or accomplishments. They just saw it as a lightning strike that would airlift them out of their mundane and messy and mad lives. And to prove their case, they could point to a long list of stars who found fame and fortune in some way through social media or reality television, from Justin Bieber to Cardi B.

I've been working with and around celebrities for many years now, and even I didn't see this coming, the explosion of celebrity obsession. But I certainly see the other side of it, the real lives behind the curtain. I have many famous people as clients, and I see up close the dangers, pain, and disappointments that come with extreme fame. I am speaking from personal experience when I testify that fame is far from a panacea. Celebrities get caught up in the same rat race as everyone else, chasing the next level of stardom or wealth. They too are desperately trying to find happiness, believing the next big movie or top-selling album will be the thing that makes their lives perfect. Magical. Even with them, the chase never seems to end.

I was caught in the trap, too, when I was younger, racing as fast as I could to accumulate as much as I could. What started to heal me was coming to grips with my life from God's perspective. Was this really what he wanted for me, this blind chase for possessions and power? I realized his opinion of me and my life was the only one that mattered. Everybody else was irrelevant. So when I was hanging out with Kanye West at his Beverly Hills house, I was nonplussed when he excitedly brought me to his bedroom to show me his new distraction.

"Let me show you what I have in my master bathroom!" he said.

I followed him inside the enormous bathroom. To my surprise, the walls of this dude's shower stall were actually a giant fish tank. He had exotic fish swimming all around him when he washed his behind. I could only laugh. It was funny to me, seeing the folly in trying to keep up with the Joneses (or the Wests) in a place like Beverly Hills. I thought I had a pretty nice house—but I didn't take a shower inside a damn aquarium. However, my shower, the one without the aquarium, got me just as clean.

When I first arrived in Hollywood nearly thirty years ago, I found myself standing in the living room of Dyan Cannon, the three-time Academy Award nominee who was probably best known in America for her antics during the Lakers games, where she joined celebrities like Jack Nicholson courtside as they cheered Magic Johnson and the rest of the Showtime crew on their way to five championships. Dyan, a born-again Christian, wanted me to come to her house and lead some of her friends in prayer and Bible study. At the precious age of thirty-two, I had already achieved a lofty status as a highly sought-after spiritual leader with more than a thousand speaking requests a year. My ministry was pulling in millions annually, and I employed fifteen people to stay on top of it all. But my influence had largely been in the faith world. This would be my letter of introduction to Hollywood.

Over the following months I stood in Dyan's living room as the Hollywood Walk of Fame came to life, past and future. All of them American legends, perched on chairs in Dyan's home, hanging on my every word. How many thirty-two-year-old black guys from exceedingly modest upbringings get to experience that? These were folks who had done extremely well in their careers, particularly financially, but they felt like something was missing. They were trapped in the mundane and felt a void in their souls. They needed some kind of nourishment, but they weren't sure what it was and where it would come from.

I sensed I could reach out and touch them, engage with their spirit. Show them how to hear God talking to them. Introduce magic into their lives. Imbue them with the Miracle Mentality. They began to see me as a chef for their souls, a spiritual leader who was able to step outside of the church, away from the pulpit, and deal with them in the secular world—offering the kind of encouragement and self-discovery they needed to begin to transform their lives and add real meaning.

I don't use this chef analogy lightly. In Hollywood, chefs are the ultimate status symbol. Having the pull and the money to procure a famous, high-profile chef working his or her magic in your private kitchen gives you the right to brag to any Hollywood insider. Personal chefs are even more prized than a flashy car. Celebrities are all foodies; they talk about food all day long. Actors, athletes, entertainers—they're all the same.

That's what I became—a private chef for the soul. I now call it *life coaching*, a term that wasn't yet part of our lexicon in 1992. When I began to connect with these famous people, I saw that their lives were plagued by the same patterns as everybody else's. They were in the life states of mundane, messy, and mad, trying to find magic. Even the ones I would have expected to have it all figured out. I recognized early in my spiritual career that God had given me a special talent, an ability not only to connect with people on a deep level but also to sense what was ailing them, what they needed to lift them up. It was clear the people I ministered to could sense my gift as well.

After I began connecting with celebrities at Dyan's house, they started showing up at my talks and sermons around Southern California. I'd look up and see Smokey Robinson or Stevie Wonder or Natalie Cole in the front row. After an event a guy came up to me and said, "Stevie wants to talk to you." Stevie Wonder met me in the back room, sat down, and we began to talk. Clearly he had a lot of questions he needed answered, particularly concerning the nature of faith and about his own life.

"Hey, man, I want you to come to my house," he said.

Wow, Stevie's house. That's deep, I thought.

When I arrived, Stevie made it clear he needed some food for his soul.

I had the same level of deep connection with Charlton Heston—Moses himself!—who wanted to delve into his spirituality. I would get approached in random places—restaurants, clubs, Laker games—by celebrities who needed help. Sometimes at that very moment. I saw right away that for all their successes, these people still had not found peace of mind or happiness. Worldwide fame and untold riches were not going to get them there, and they won't get you there either. In our celebrity-obsessed culture, where we think our idols have everything a human could ever want or need, I sensed this was a message most people seriously needed to hear.

If celebrities aren't happy, what does that say about the chance for happiness for the rest of us, particularly those of us who use celebrities as our gauge of success or fulfillment? Just being good at your job will never be enough. Having enough to pay your bills won't be enough. We always feel like we need more, more, more. The advent of reality TV has made it all so much worse. For a young person, fame and riches feel so close—just come up with the right gimmick, the right YouTube video, the right crazy dance, and you can hold fame and wealth in your hands and be fabulously happy. As a result of all the images you are bombarded with, the life you are actually living, what we might call *real* life, is never going to be satisfying, never going to be enough. Everything will feel mundane compared to the Kardashians. And I am here to tell you, fame and fortune will never be a path to the magical, until you discover your true identity, the things you were put here to do.

I mentioned earlier that I grew up in a house where there was not a lot of magic. We didn't have a lot of money, my parents were not well-educated, and there always seemed to be mayhem and drama swirling around the house I shared with my parents and four siblings. My father was a steelworker and my mother worked in a doughnut shop. There was very little affection between them, and at times the inside of the house felt like a cold garage. But there was something else that contributed to the messiness and madness for me, and it would take my father's death for me to discover the shocking reality of my existence.

During the first twelve years of my life, I always felt slightly off-kilter in my family, like I wasn't exactly flying in the same direction as the rest of the flock. I was the bird who veered left too quickly or who faced the wrong way on the telephone wire. A lot of it stemmed from my skin color. My mother, who is Spanish, has a light olive complexion; if you looked quickly you might mistake her for a very light-skinned black woman. My father was also light, but undoubtedly Spanish. All four of my siblings looked very Spanish. My parents and siblings had green eyes and silky hair.

Then there was me. Not dark, but definitely not like I was just Spanish, with my brown eyes and hair that stubbornly refused to lay down like everybody else's.

When we all were out in public, I stood out like a fly in a sugar bowl.

"Oh my gosh, you have the most beautiful family," a waitress once said as she showed us to our seats. Then she turned to me. "Who's *this* little kid?"

Yes, that actually happened. Over and over, some version of the same scene played out. The Mexican barber who cut my brother's and my hair would complain loudly, "How the hell did you get this hair?" he said, looking down at my unruly mane. "Maaaann! It's fighting against me!"

At least once a year I'd go with my siblings up to Seattle to spend time with my cousins. My aunt was a pretty Latin lady who married a very good-looking black man who was quite dark, so their kids were mixed. Any observer would quickly see that they looked like me, but I was oblivious to the similarities. I loved going to Seattle because my eyes were opened to a world I knew nothing about: a black world—hip music, cool dances, flashy jump rope. When I was five or six, these older female cousins said to me, "Timmy, you're one of us, but we can't tell you the whole story." I had no idea what they were talking about.

When I was eleven, I was devastated when my father was killed. His death shook our family to the core; none of us was ever the same. A few months later, my aunt Grace visited us in Southern California. Grace was the kind of woman who enjoyed coloring outside the lines.

"I'm going to tell you something," she said to me one day when we were alone. "You deserve to know."

I liked Aunt Grace, so I listened closely.

"I think it's unfair that you're treated the way you are."

She paused and looked in my eyes. "Did you ever notice that you were left at home when your brother and sisters went somewhere special with your dad?"

I nodded. "Yes. But I don't think about it too much."

"Did you ever notice that your dad didn't spend much one-on-one time with you?"

I nodded. I was always an optimistic kid, and I'd never wanted to have negative thoughts about my father—especially a few months after he was killed.

"Timmy, have you ever thought he wasn't your dad?"

I felt a tightening in my chest, but I wanted to be strong. "Yes, Aunt Grace," I said, "but I don't really want to talk about it."

"No, you need to know about it," she said, shaking her head. "I don't know if I'll ever get to have this conversation with you again."

She methodically laid out for me her understanding of the dramatic origins of my life. I think she felt a sense of urgency because she was about to get divorced from my uncle and possibly would never see me again. It turns out she was right about that; I never saw her again after that afternoon. But her words transformed my life.

She said my mother and father had had some rocky times during their marriage. Rumor had it my father had gone outside of their marriage, so Grace said my mother decided to respond by doing the same. My mother had a relationship with a light-skinned black man who played in a band, and she got pregnant. When I was born and clearly looked like I was part black, there was a family crisis. But my parents decided to stay together.

I later confirmed that what she told me was true—the man I had presumed was my father was not my father at all. While the news was extremely unsettling, it also quickly blossomed into an enormous awakening. It took about five minutes for me to move from recovery mode to discovery mode. I thought about my family relationships and realized this news explained so much of what I had observed over the years. No wonder my brother occasionally talked down to me during intense arguments. He was nice to me, but he could be condescending. No wonder my older sister acted like she felt sorry for me. It was confusing because I felt like I was a top dog in my world, a Little League star who was the envy of many kids in the neighborhood. *Why did she always sound like she pitied me?*

I had discovered in an instant that I was the family's black sheep. But rather than devastate me, the news liberated me. I even thought about my television viewing—now I understood why I was so excited by the music and dancing I saw on *Soul Train* while nobody else in the family seemed to care when it came on Saturday mornings.

The next time I went to Seattle I dove headfirst into the world of my cousins. After needling me about my unruly hair, they took me to a hair care store—where I was thrilled to see for the first time the products like Afro Sheen that were advertised on *Soul Train*—and bought me a rake to comb my hair. My cousins taught me how to dance—and I discovered I was good at it. I had rhythm. And I must admit, I was much better than my siblings.

I didn't confront my mother with my news, but she grew extremely uncomfortable when she saw the rake in my pocket when I came back from Seattle.

"Be careful, Timmy," she said. "People will see you with that and it won't make a good impression."

In other words, people would see me with the rake and assume I was black.

My mother could tell I was onto something, so she started feeding me fabricated family tales.

"What you don't know," she said, "is that you have an uncle you've never met who looks exactly like you."

I would look at her quizzically, waiting to see what else she was going to make up.

Around this time I went to a black barbershop for the first time to get my hair cut. I looked around in amazement, soaking up the talk, the jokes, the little kids waiting. It felt like I was in a movie, a bright, exciting world vividly come to life.

I sat down in the barber's chair and he went to work without me saying a word about what I wanted. He knew exactly what to do.

"Man, you're a good-looking brother!" he said as he buzzed around my head with the clippers. "You look like a little movie star. Where you from? You're not from around here."

He put some oily liquid on my head that smelled like a burst of sunshine. "You get your butt back here and I'll take care of you," he said as I stepped down off the chair.

I walked out of that shop a transformed person. I had never been called good-looking. I had never been in a place where I felt so comfortable, so natural. The man who cut my hair was a far cry from the complaining Mexican barber. I felt like I had found my home.

I was starting to discover some magic in my origins. However, I still carried a certain heaviness around with me for a long time. I think this happens to many of us when we have painful incidents from our childhoods that we'd rather forget.

When I went to a therapist after I entered my thirties, one of the most impactful questions she asked me during my five years on her couch was, "How does it feel to not be yourself?"

Through our digging, we discovered I had chosen to pursue a lofty status in the church after graduating from Southeastern University in Florida mainly because I was looking for a place where I fit in. Clearly this was a remnant from the discoveries of my childhood. I was now grown up, but I was still wanting to be accepted, welcomed, embraced. Although I didn't feel comfortable with all the church doctrines, I was willing to go along to get along. I would smile a lot when the people around me used words of condemnation to advance the church's conservative orthodoxy against homosexuality. I didn't think gay people were all going to hell, but I didn't want to incite any confrontation.

I was staying in fancy suites, driving nice cars, employing a large staff—though to the consternation of my board members, I was taking a modest salary from a ministry that was annually bringing in several million. I was running around with some of the biggest names in Hollywood and business—thirty-two years old and calling men like Charlton Heston, James Caan, Vidal Sassoon, and Lee Iacocca my friends. These guys had run out of things to talk about, so they'd look at me and ask, "Hey, Tim, what's going on with young people?" And I'd hold court for hours, cracking them up with jokes and spellbinding stories.

When I walked into a party in Beverly Hills I was usually the only black person in the room—often the only one within miles. Yeah, Prince lived down the road, but usually it was just me. I was allowed in their space because I was charismatic and they thought I brought them an aura of cool, as if it could rub off on them. Honestly, it felt a lot like high school.

I knew in my soul that I wasn't in the place I should be. On the surface I appeared to be riding high, but inside I felt off. I felt like I was faking. I needed some sort of transformation, but I didn't know what that should look like.

Not long ago I took my eighty-nine-year-old mother to lunch. (She was born in 1931.) She likes to go to a diner in Whittier, where they still serve the same food they've had on the menu since I was a kid. Whenever we go, she orders the same thing.

One time I asked her, "Mom, don't you want to order something else?"

She said, "No, I know what I like," and then she laughed. I admired her answer, because she's okay with herself. She is who she is. She doesn't have to apologize or feel like she has to order something different for the sake of pleasing someone else. She knows what she likes. She's lived a long time and been through too much to feel as though she owes anybody anything.

It took years for me to start the process of understanding myself. I had to be brave enough to start anew, this time on *a foundation of truth*. Spirituality will always be an important part of my life, but I discovered I had many tools in my kit to help people. By standing squarely in front of the mirror and not running away from what I saw, I was able to profoundly change the man I am. I knew I had the gift to heal, to help people through their ailments and their pain by helping them tap into the power of God. I knew I needed to go toward that power, embracing it, reveling in it. That's who I was. I had found the magic.

The process of self-discovery is one I have engineered for many of my clients. We are all anointed in some way, gifted by a higher power with a calling. We all are able to access supernatural strength, to bring about transformation—to make miracles happen for us. But we can't stay closed off and turn our backs on this ability. We have to listen, to slow down and hear what God is telling us. We must have a Miracle Mentality if we are going to bring transformation into our lives. It's sitting right there in our heads, just waiting for us to reach inside and access it. The time to start is now. Right now.

Trapped vs. Stalled

When I talk to people about their lives, I often hear them throw out one of two words to describe their condition: *trapped* or *stalled*. I'd like to break down these two states of being.

I often hear people describe themselves as *trapped* when I

travel around the country and speak to the young ladies at the Paul Mitchell schools. In many of the smaller cities of the Midwest, as many as 80 percent of them might raise their hands if I ask how many of them feel trapped.

I'm more likely to hear *stalled* when I work with some of my high-powered corporate clients in life-coaching sessions or when people are talking about their careers. We will discuss this in much greater detail in chapter 7, but being stalled indicates you have reached some sort of plateau. Perhaps you experienced success earlier in your career and your forward or upward momentum seems to have ceased. No more promotions, no more raises, no more exciting assignments. You are stuck in the mundane—and you have no idea or plan for how to get out of it.

To be trapped is to be confined, to be held, to be kept. To be stalled is to be temporarily not moving. In that sense, stalled is better than trapped, because when you're stalled you feel like maybe you can get moving again if you get some gas or a push. When you're trapped, you literally can't see a way out of your predicament.

If we look at it through the lens of Maslow's hierarchy of needs,[1] people who are stalled and those who are trapped are at two very different stages. For those who aren't familiar with the much-quoted theory, American psychologist Abraham Maslow formulated a way of looking at human motivation that had a much more positive framework than most previous work in the field, which tended to focus on abnormalities and illness.

Maslow's hierarchy, first published in 1943, suggested that human motivation is focused on a search for fulfillment and change through personal growth. Usually constructed on a pyramid, the most elemental needs on the bottom rung are basic or physiological: food, water, sleep, sex, homeostasis, and excretion. The next level is safety needs: security, order, health, and stability. The third level is love and belonging. The fourth is esteem—the need to be competent and recognized, such as through status and level of success. At the top of the pyramid is the need for self-actualization, when individuals reach a state of harmony and understanding because they are engaged in achieving their full potential.

Maslow's general idea was that we need to satisfy most of the needs on each level before we can move up to the next one. For instance, when we were all sheltering in place during the coronavirus pandemic, the entire globe was stuck on the second level: safety needs. When you feel trapped, you are much closer to the lower level needs, such as safety.

The word *trapped* implies there is a ceiling above you, limiting your growth. When I talked to the Paul Mitchell students on a recent trip, I told them, "Look up." All heads rose to look up at the ceiling.

"Look at the height of that ceiling," I said. "If I let go of a helium balloon, it can go that high and stop. The question is, how high is the ceiling in your house? How high is the ceiling in the relationship you're in with the person you're with? How high is the ceiling in your own mind? Because you're going to be confined by that ceiling."

Parents are a major factor in how high the ceiling rises for their children. Those of you who were lucky enough to have parents who raised you to soar to the heavens were able to access a Miracle Mentality from a young age. Perhaps you were lucky enough to retain it as you got older. As I will discuss in chapter 4, parents play a pivotal role in this equation.

I would like to close this chapter with a few lyrics from a Stevie Wonder masterpiece. As I mentioned earlier, I have had the fortune to get to know Stevie over the years, and I can testify that his entire life has been defined by the Miracle Mentality. From the classic album *Songs in the Key of Life*, the song "If It's Magic" is Stevie's paean to the power of love.

> "If it's magic
> Why can't we make it everlasting?"

CHAPTER 3

Activating the Magical

Now that I've made my case that it *is* possible for you to access a Miracle Mentality, you're probably asking, *Okay, smart guy, how do I get to the magic? How can I activate the Miracle Mentality in my life?*

Let me be clear: miracles don't usually happen miraculously. It's likely going to take some work to get to there. It's going to take some work to develop a Miracle Mentality, and given the explosion of social media, today it will require even more effort. As we talked about earlier, too many people imagine that fame and fortune will come their way due to the power of Instagram or Twitter or YouTube—if they can just get a certain number of likes and followers, they'll be discovered, and their life will be full of the miraculous. It's fascinating to me how much we have allowed these platforms to infiltrate our lives without doing a serious assessment of how much they might alter our society, impact our children, even change our brains. It would be like distributing a drug to every person in the country above age ten without any prior testing or approval from the FDA.

So I think we need to set aside the idea that social media is your path to the magic. None of us has the exact same path from the mundane or messy to the magic because none of us are in exactly the same place. But I think there are universal principles that can be helpful.

How to Activate a Miracle Mentality

To step into the magical, you need a healthy dollop of talent, opportunity, and desire. You can have two of them, but missing that third will often keep you stuck in the mundane or messy. For instance, how many of us know someone with plenty of talent and desire, but who hasn't yet had the opportunity to demonstrate their talent to people who can bring about change for them? Or someone who may have access to opportunity and have the desire to get there, but just doesn't have the talent or ability to pull it off? But when those three elements come together, look out for the fireworks. There are so many examples we can use to illustrate this equation.

For instance, Whitney Houston was the child of an extremely talented singer, Cissy Houston, and the cousin of Dionne Warwick, who isn't too shabby herself, so she grew up deeply embedded in the music industry. This gave her plenty of opportunities that weren't available to other young black girls in Essex County, New Jersey. Her mother had toiled for many years as a backup singer, and she filled her daughter with the desire to reach the stardom that had eluded Cissy. But does anyone believe Whitney would have become one of the most popular singers of all time if she hadn't been blessed with that magnificent talent?

I come across many young people who are praying for fame and riches, thinking they are missing the opportunity. But what are you going to be famous for? What are you working on that will bring you this fame? What are you pouring into yourself? I see too much desire in search of opportunity, leaving out that last essential element in the equation—talent—which gets too little attention.

Please understand, when I mention the word *talent*, I'm not just talking about the obvious things, like Whitney Houston's fantastic singing ability or Jamie Foxx's incredible gift for impersonations and acting. I'm talking about finding your passion—the miracle that's resting, waiting, inside of you. About you recognizing the thing God specifically created you to manifest. You know, the thing you always knew you could do better than everybody else around you or the thing that always brought you great joy. Those talents and passions were a manifestation of God whispering in your ear, telling you this was what you were created to do. It's the miracle inside of you.

When I'm traveling to smaller towns across America, people often tell me they feel trapped because of where they live. *Can somebody still have a magical life in Lexington, Kentucky?* The answer is a resounding yes. Activating the magic has no connection to where you live. In all honesty, for somebody like a Paul Mitchell student, it may be a lot easier to find success in a place like Lexington than it would be in Los Angeles. Just imagine how many hairstylists are trying to make a go of it in LA, joining the legions of others who have made their way to the City of Angels looking to become the next Paul Mitchell. Contrast that with the hairstyling scene in Lexington. In which place would it be easier to make a big splash showing women how to be the most beautiful versions of themselves? I say Lexington, by a mile—the proverbial big fish in a small pond. Those women in Lexington desperately need you. LA? Not so much. But to access a taste of magic in Lexington requires turning off the Kardashians and readjusting the way you are seeing your town.

What I often see—in both Lexington and LA—is the strong, debilitating presence of fear. *What if I try and I don't make it? I will have confirmed my worst fears about myself.* I understand the way that works. We all have to fight off fear at certain times in our lives. In the backs of our minds, we are grappling with the paralysis it can bring. If you take the chance, you are opening yourself up to the possibility of failure. It's a lot safer to just keep running in place. Or take a seat and not even try.

Often corrosive memories from our past are getting in the way. Fear transports us to the moment when it began to make sense to us to protect ourselves from disappointment. Perhaps you were an eight-year-old girl, dressed in a brand-new outfit, waiting eagerly by the door for your father to pick you up and take you to the zoo. And once again it looks like he isn't showing up. You keep checking your reflection in the mirror, making sure you look perfect for Daddy. After a while you stop looking out the window. You try to watch television, but you can't concentrate. You're trying not to breathe too loud, believing you might miss the knock on the door.

When your dad doesn't show up, once again, you either conclude that he's a monster or that it was a mistake for you to put all that hope in this good thing happening for you. To prevent the crushing disappointment from revisiting you, on that day you conclude that putting hope into people, into situations, into things working out for you, is a dangerous gamble. Life is so much easier if you just shut all of that down. You vow you will never open yourself up again to the pain you felt that night, to the tears that dampened your pillow as you cried yourself to sleep. You basically close off a section of your heart—the section where hope resided.

In that moment you make it much harder to access the magic, to take chances, to think you are capable of scaling that next big obstacle.

As we discuss activating the magic in our lives, I need to stress that each of us has been magically made and magically mastered by God. Ephesians 2:10 says, "For we are God's handiwork, created in Christ Jesus to do good works, which God prepared in advance for us to do" (NIV). Jeremiah 18:6 makes a similar point when the Lord tells Jeremiah that he is the potter and we are the clay, and he shapes us in whatever way he deems best, just as the potter does for the piece of pottery he is creating. If you think of yourself as clay in the hands of the Lord, it's easy to imagine that he has placed the magic inside of you. Your job is to let the magic out, to let it start transforming your life. The path to transformation is by education, observation, and conversation. These are present in every case of transformation I have ever seen—including in my own life.

When I was in sixth grade, I came across a book about the life of Michelangelo, and my mind took off. I was astounded by the sheer creativity and genius of this man considered by many to be the greatest artist of all time. He opened up my mind to all kinds of possibilities for my own life—the possibility for my life to be filled with magic.

My next example is a bit more materialistic but still important in my development. Under the category of observation, when I sat in a big, fancy Mercedes sedan for the first time and heard the doors close with a soft whisper that sounded like a caress, I thought, *Wow! I didn't know they made cars like this!* From that day forward, I knew that whatever I did in my life, I had to have one of those cars. It became a driving force for me—and I was thrilled when I bought my first Mercedes. I should add that the thrill of owning one didn't last nearly as long as I thought it would. After all, even though it was a fine automobile, it's just a car. Cars can seem magical, but they're not going to transform your life.

To give you an example of the transformative power of conversation, I go back to the conversations I was having with older, wiser guys when I first started moving around Hollywood. Men like Quincy Jones really changed the way I looked at the world and my place in it. Quincy started calling me "The Voice," claiming that just as he had created the "King of Pop" sobriquet for Michael Jackson, he was giving me that nickname because I had a unique ability as a sort of "pop prophet," gauging the state of popular culture and providing much-needed sustenance for our collective souls. His words were like a powerful talisman for me, giving me confidence and the resolve to move among his crowd.

If we know each of us has been masterfully made, then we begin to understand that every day we wake up breathing is a magical day, filled with possibilities. And we think more deeply about our personal definition of magic and how it already shows up in our lives.

I know of a young man who was in a serious car accident that paralyzed him from the waist down. When you step into his presence, you immediately notice his zest for life, his light that seems to shine from within.

"How long have you been paralyzed?" I asked him.

"Nine years," he said.

"I'm curious—on a scale of one to ten, how do you see your life?"

"Nine," he answered.

"Wow, that high?" I questioned. "Even after the accident and all of that?"

"Oh man, I'm so grateful to be alive," he said with a smile. "I can see. I have my family. I've experienced so many things. Tim, I realized I just gotta deal with this part of my life, but the other things I still enjoy. As a matter of fact, I enjoy them even more."

His explanation brings to the fore the idea that *magic* can mean so many different things to different people. It's entirely relative to your situation. For one person, introducing magic into his life might mean being able to work from home so that he can spend more time with his kids. For another, it might be having the time to read more books, or finishing that college degree, or getting to the theater more often.

You start with the small things that are within your reach but that can bring enormous value to your life. Once you begin to do that, you will be amazed by how much it opens the portal to larger, grander magical experiences. You don't need to become Beyoncé or Kim Kardashian to start accessing magic. Really, you just need a path to hope and joy. That book you bring home from the library might unleash some dormant talent or hobby that can change everything. Little by little, those small pieces of magic start stringing together into bigger things. One day you look up and realize your life isn't the same. You can see a beautiful bright light at the end of the tunnel—and you no longer feel it's the headlights of a speeding train hurtling toward you. The speckles of magic begin to be sprinkled in every corner of your life, bringing about changes that make you a happier, more pleasant person. People who are close to you wonder where the glow is coming from—and the glow starts spreading to your children, your family members, your significant other. Or if you're single, you begin to attract a much different kind of potential partner. And it all started with a very small change, a little sprinkling of magic dust.

Before I show you how you can transform the different areas of your life and access the Miracle Mentality, I'd like to make one more point.

Relax.

I use that word often when I'm speaking to different groups.

During one of my Paul Mitchell meetings, a young lady was expressing to me how depressing and hopeless her life was.

"Relax," I said to her. "There may be more magic around you than you realize. But calm down. Take deep breaths. Look at what you have instead of what you don't have."

When I said that, she immediately started sobbing.

She came up to me afterward and said, "Oh my God, it's like you just set me free. There's magic in my grandkids. I keep thinking, I didn't do it. I didn't make it. I'm already fifty-five years of age. I didn't do it. But when you said to relax, I realized there really was more magic around me than I thought."

As you set out on the path to magic, to the Miracle Mentality, by reading through these pages, I want you to note the place you're starting. Look around you. Take it all in. When you hit moments of frustration and impatience on your journey—moments that are inevitable—you will be able to look back and see how far you've already gone. You'll recognize your progress, your growth, and your stages of meaningful transformation. And you will rejoice not only in moving toward your destination, you will celebrate the journey itself.

CHAPTER 4

Parenting

Parenting brings with it a dizzying rush of daily stressors and mini heart attacks. Seemingly every day we're making crucial decisions by the seat of our pants, with little information and even less expertise. It can take years before we even know whether we have done it right. When broken down to the basics, the job of a parent is to guide, guard, and govern their child. If one of these isn't done adequately, the child is going to suffer in untold ways, likely well into their adulthood.

As generations of therapists and developmental psychologists have noted, parents who fail at these three responsibilities often were not properly guided, guarded, and governed themselves when they were a child. This stuff tends to come back and repeat itself with a vengeance, as nasty as a Jason attack in *Friday the 13th*.

To be clear, *guide* means direction, *guard* refers to protection, and *govern* is administration. In my travels I constantly come across adults who are suffering because their childhood was missing one—or in some unfortunate cases, more than one—of these qualities.

At a Paul Mitchell school in the Midwest, a young woman raised her hand during my talk. I saw tears rolling down her face.

"Tim, I never had a chance at the Miracle Mentality," she said. "My mother had me with just-a-boyfriend, and as I was growing up, she would switch from boyfriend to boyfriend to boyfriend. All I saw was mess."

This girl was only twenty and she had already resigned herself to being trapped in a life without magic. It was a reminder that if parents don't find a way to get out of the mess and the madness, they're going to pass it down to the next generation. There is a relevant phrase we use in Christian circles: "reverse the curse." If we have been burdened with trauma and madness from our parents, one of our most important jobs will be to make sure that cycle ends with us. We must do everything within our power to bring up our children with the Miracle Mentality, to give them a chance at a happy, productive, healthy life.

Psalm 78 is the Bible's love offering to parents, giving an exhaustive accounting of the miracles of God, the deeds he has performed, so that the next generation will know about the things of God and they in turn can tell their children. In the biblical construction, we're always looking three generations down; your actions will affect your children's children. A message I often teach is that we have to learn not only to believe in miracles ourselves but to teach our children to expect miracles. Once they have learned how to receive miracles, then we teach them to release miracles out into the world.

That may sound like a level of maturity so advanced that no one could ever possibly meet it, but I have seen it in action. For instance, one of my friends, Bobby Shriver, is the son of Eunice and Sargent

Shriver. The Shrivers are one of the great American families, with an incredible legacy of service. Eunice was the sister of President John Kennedy, and during Kennedy's first term, Sargent founded the Peace Corps. Sargent and Eunice had five children, including Bobby and Maria Shriver, who was married for over thirty years to Arnold Schwarzenegger.

Bobby and I had a fascinating conversation one day, and he told me his parents worked hard to ingrain in the children the requirement that they must pass generosity on to others. It was a family expectation. As a result, each of them has a special relationship with miracles—they believe, expect, receive, and become miracles in their own lives. Each of the children is deeply involved in nonprofits, and each has done considerable work over the years on behalf of others. That family is a miracle in the lives of so many people, they are in effect releasing miracles into the world. The Shrivers have demonstrated it is possible for an entire family to possess the Miracle Mentality. But it all starts with parents who make it a priority.

Mundane Parenting

What does it look like when a parent is stuck in the mundane?

As I stated earlier, the mundane is the ordinary, the common, the status quo. It's the daily routine, the regular, the steady. All good, right? Certainly, there's nothing wrong with having a steady routine. But the mundane has stages. It starts out as a routine, your regular schedule, but then it can lead to boredom, and boredom can lead to frustration. And that's where the problems start. When a parent begins to parent their children from that place of frustration, things start to go bad. Mothers and fathers begin to pass on that emotion to the children and a chill settles over the entire household. The children start staying away, spending as much time as they can outside the house—often in places where trouble is sitting right next to them, waiting to be taken for a spin.

How does the mundane cross into dangerous territory? How do we know when our everyday routines have veered from comforting to problematic?

I saw a vivid and painful illustration recently of the mundane unsettling the parental realm. I got invited to a birthday party for the six-year-old child of a friend. The party was taking place at Chuck E. Cheese, a restaurant that brought back many memories of when my kids were small. As I walked in, I was greeted by a bevy of attractive moms standing around and talking, idling as parents tend to do at kiddie birthday parties.

"Oooh, I love Chuck E. Cheese," I said as I waded into the group.

"Why?" all eight of them said at the same time, with a disbelieving tone.

"I don't know—I just love it," I said.

"Well, when was the last time you came?" one of them asked me.

I thought for a second. "Oh, probably about ten years ago."

Another rolled her eyes. "Well, I've been to seven parties here in three months," she said with an exasperated sigh.

They explained that everybody scheduled their parties at Chuck E. Cheese because it was a turn-key operation for six-year-olds. The parents handed over payment and the Chuck E. Cheese folks did everything else—the pizza, the tickets, the games, the birthday cake. And then Chuck E. came out to entertain the little ones. *Done.*

"Ladies, how long does this take?" I asked.

The whole production could be done in about ninety minutes, they agreed. "We got here at twelve. We'll be out by one thirty," one of them said. Then she looked at me with a grimace spreading across her face. "Chuck E. Cheese is the ultimate birth control." She shook her head, her voice dripping with sarcasm. "This place has made me not ever want to have another child!"

I chuckled, but I walked away thinking the Chuck E. Cheese birthday party was the ultimate symbol of the mundane. Even six-year-olds probably get bored with a Chuck E. Cheese party twice a month. The first one probably felt magical. By the seventh one, the pizza is tasting a bit stale.

Let's take a look at another example, in this case a hypothetical schoolteacher who just *loves* the second graders in her charge. She can't wait to get to school every morning to greet them with big hugs and smiles. They keep her thoroughly entertained throughout the day with their seven-year-old shenanigans. At home, she spends hours every night with her lesson plans, devising clever ways to teach and engage her class. Her excitement about her job spills over to her interactions with her own kids, whom she keeps enthralled by the wonder of learning. This goes on for several years; she's so grateful she has a job she finds fulfilling.

But then she starts having revelations. She realizes how far she has to drive every morning and evening to get to and from the school. She doesn't really like driving. The commute didn't bother her in the beginning; now it does. The little idiosyncrasies of second graders that she found adorable in the beginning start to get on her last nerve. How did she not notice before how sloppy and needy they are? The mundane has hit boredom—and, like a virus, is moving fast into the territory of frustration. She stops working so hard on the lesson plans, reusing activities from previous years. She doesn't feel like making her lunch in the morning anymore, trying to snag a few more minutes under the covers so she can summon the will to face the arduous commute and the screaming horde of seven-year-olds. She gets on the scale one morning and is shocked to discover she has put on nearly twenty pounds. The weight gain has made her feel sluggish, and she is tiring more easily in the afternoon. She's racing to her car as soon as the final bell sounds, practically knocking little ones out of her way. The other teachers observe her change in attitude with a knowing nod; they, too, have been exactly where she is. Her new demeanor has clear implications: her students don't learn as much as they used to. They grow frustrated more easily. They act out more in class. As a result, she begins to hate her job.

What's that second-grade teacher like now when she gets home to her own kids? Certainly not the patient, loving, enthusiastic mom she used to be. Her frustration and impatience bleed over into her parenting. Just as her students at school react in negative ways, so do her own children. And it all builds upon itself in a vicious cycle.

We could replace the second-grade teacher with a computer programmer, corporate lawyer, newspaper reporter . . . The patterns and the results are similar: implosion.

Mundane to Magical

How do we get from the mundane to the magical in parenting our kids?

The first step is to understand that your parenting patience, your parenting energy, your parenting creativity stem directly from how you are feeling about the state of your life. We know we don't give our kids the level of attention and care they deserve when we are unhappy with our lives. It's like the admonition we get from flight attendants at the start of a flight: *Please put the oxygen mask over your own face before you put it over your child's.*

In other words, you have to take care of your own needs properly if you are going to be an effective parent.

When you find yourself stuck in the mundane, you must take immediate action before it turns into boredom. You have to make room for the magic every week or you'll be in trouble. What is the magic? It can be something small or big. Giving magic some attention is what's important. You could do something as simple as scheduling an exciting lunch date with a colleague or friend at least once a week, where each time you go to a new restaurant. Even the process of doing the research to figure out where you will eat can add excitement and energy to your week. You might take a yoga class once or twice a week to help you stay centered and give you some physical activity to look forward to. Perhaps you can learn a new skill or take up a new hobby. Tennis. Bowling. Crocheting. Gardening. Building and caring for bonsai plants. The possibilities are endless.

In my life coaching I find that recreation is the area we neglect the most. A typical life-coaching session might go something like this:

"On a scale of one to ten, how's your clarity, your mindset? How you are feeling?" I ask. "Do you feel peace in your mind? Do you experience clarity?"

"Oh, maybe about a seven. I feel distracted a lot," they'll say.

"Okay, on a scale of one to ten, how do you feel in your spiritual life? Whatever faith you are, do you feel a connection to the source?"

"I'd give that a five. I feel like I've been too busy," they might say.

"How are you with your job?" I'll ask.

"Not great," they'll say. "That's a three."

"How about your finances?"

"Ah, that could be better. Five."

"How are you with your family time?"

This usually gets a grimace. "I haven't been spending enough time with them. Maybe a four."

Then the next question always blows them away. "How are you with your recreation and hobbies?"

Most overachievers will look at me with a frown, almost as if they don't understand the question. "What do you mean, recreation? Hobbies?"

They'll shake their head. "I don't know. I'm so busy. I've got too much going on."

Recreation is the area that in many ways can impact all the others the most but to which we pay the least amount of attention. You have to be intentional about it. Schedule things you know you will enjoy—just you, not you and your daughter, or you and your significant other. Something that's just for you. When you start to do that, your mundane lifestyle will be injected with a healthy dose of magic, which will soon bleed into your parenting. Your children will be the immediate beneficiaries.

Messy

One of my life-coaching clients is an extremely successful middle-aged businessman. He's made a great deal of money over the years. But unfortunately his business requires him to travel overseas all the time, to look after his company and his two hundred employees. It didn't take long for the thing that was making him very, very rich to make him very poor in his family. One of his children was excelling in school, but his other child was spiraling in drug addiction. This man knew his inattention to his family, the lack of time he spent with his children, had created a mess that was threatening the entire family structure. But he didn't see how he could change.

He told his wife, "Babe, I gotta keep going if we want to live like this, if we want a house like this, if we want NFL season tickets."

For a while she nodded and accepted his argument. "Okay, okay, I get it."

But as she saw her family crumbling, his frequent absences started to wear on her. The addiction of the older child was affecting the younger one, sending that child into a deep depression, even to the point of contemplating suicide. The wife began to wonder, *Where's my husband who's supposed to be guiding, guarding, and governing the family?* The family's mess had become untenable. The father came to me, asking what he could do to stop the ship from sinking.

A big plus in this man's favor was that he at least recognized his family was in a messy state. Many families have been in the mess for so long, they don't even see the walls crumbling around them. When I was nine years old, one day I went into the house of a kid down the street who was a frequent playmate of mine. It was the first time I'd stepped foot in the house—and I was shocked by how nasty it was. They had three dogs, and I saw dog poop on the floor. Yet they walked around as if they couldn't see it. Or smell it! The couch was covered in a layer of dog hair. *All the time.* I was so disgusted; I didn't understand how anyone could live like that. I came from a home that was exceedingly neat and orderly because that's what my mother demanded. I wasn't used to that level of inattention to basic hygiene. When I went into the kitchen, I saw a sink overflowing with dirty dishes. I watched the family members closely and could tell no one was bothered by the mess. They had grown so accustomed to it that they didn't even notice.

They were like that guy we've all encountered who walks around in a cloud of his own body funk. He just stinks up every room he enters, oblivious to the effect he has on people.

I didn't know that family down the street very well, so I'm not really sure how the mess affected the mindset of the family members.

But I'm quite certain getting used to such an extreme level of nastiness had to have an impact on the family's mental health. When kids are raised in a messy environment, they get used to a certain amount of disorder. Things always seem to be in a state of flux. Nobody is responsible for cleaning up after themselves. They rarely eat dinner together at the table; they rarely talk to each other or ask how the day went. A kind of selfishness is at work: everybody is doing their own thing, minding their own business, unconcerned about how their actions impact others.

Keeping a clean house, a clean space, is part of a social contract. It's something parents are constantly reminding their children about, the responsibility they have to others. When that contract is ignored, everyone's mental health begins to suffer.

Psychologists have conducted numerous studies that reveal the link between messy or chaotic spaces and the adverse effect it has on your health. A 2010 study by researchers at the University of California found that couples who described their house as messy had increased levels of cortisol, the hormone our bodies produce in response to stress. Women were more adversely affected than men.[1] An Indiana University study of black families in St. Louis found that people with clean homes are generally healthier than people with messy homes. The researchers determined that house cleanliness was a stronger predictor of physical health than factors like neighborhood walkability.[2] When kids live in messy spaces—even though they may fight any parental efforts to make them clean—they have a more difficult time focusing on tasks such as schoolwork, according to experts. Clutter makes everyone more irritable, anxious, and frustrated, which can lead to damaged relationships.

A writer friend of mine who was married to another writer went with his wife on a couples' therapy weekend so that they could write about the experience for a national magazine. He said he was somewhat skeptical about whether the weekend would be useful at all. He didn't think they were having any major problems in their marriage that needed addressing. But over the course of the two days they both had a startling revelation.

Tension had been growing in their household over the cleanliness of the spaces. They hadn't reached a crisis stage yet, but it was bubbling beneath the surface. She was annoyed because she felt like he didn't do enough to keep the living room space clean and free of the clutter of mail piled up on the counter. He was annoyed because he felt like she did an inadequate job of keeping her clothes, her shoes, and her books from cluttering up their bedroom.

During the therapy weekend, they went through exercises that asked them to go back to their childhoods. This led them to a fascinating discovery. He realized that when he was a child, his mother didn't give him any cleaning responsibilities for the common areas of the house, but she insisted that he keep his room immaculate. His wife had the opposite requirement: she was responsible for cleaning the common areas of the house every Saturday morning before she could do anything else, but her mother didn't care whether her own room was messy or not.

Fast-forward two decades. They realized their disagreements over the cleanliness of their home had a direct connection to their childhoods. He liked a clean bedroom; she insisted on a clean living room and dining room. The two sides fit together like the pieces of a little puzzle. Much of the antagonism and blame they had been directing toward the other partner dissipated almost instantly. It was like a pressure valve had been released. The lesson: our childhood experiences can have an enormous impact on our lives as adults, in almost every area.

Sometimes we don't find out the huge impact our parents have on our state of mind until they're gone. Losing a parent can be the trigger that tosses us into a messy state. I made that discovery with my friend Kanye West.

I met Kanye for the first time during a long flight from Los Angeles to Miami. As I settled into my seat, I fervently hoped the person occupying the seat next to me was not going to be annoying or unpleasant. I think we've probably all said that silent prayer—calling on the Almighty to intervene just for a second and repel any crying babies or overly talkative morons. Perhaps the Almighty heard me because I got a shock when I saw who actually *was* sitting next to me in first class: Kanye West.

I saw him step onto the plane and glance up at the seat numbers. When he settled down in the aisle seat right next to me, I purposely didn't react. I've been around celebrities long enough to know that the worst move to make is to be a fan boy up in someone's face. Kanye probably sent up the same quick prayer when he got on the plane: *Please, Lord, don't let me be sitting next to somebody annoying!* Kanye's so creative, his prayer probably sounded like a rap verse.

I didn't want to disturb Kanye so I ignored him. I kept reading my *USA Today* and never looked in his direction.

Now, it's one thing to be up in a celebrity's face, making him uncomfortable with your excessive worship. But it's another thing to *ignore* him. Kayne West didn't seem to appreciate being ignored.

"Hey, man," he said to me as the plane was taking off.

I glanced over at him. "How you doin'?"

"Do you know who I am?" he asked.

"Yeah," I said. Then I went back to reading the newspaper.

After a tiny pause, Kanye said, "Why didn't you say anything?"

"I'm just giving you your space," I responded.

That was all it took to crank open the floodgates. It turned out to be a transformative five-hour flight for both of us. We talked about art, music, and religion. Kanye had never heard of me, but when he found out what I did, who I worked with in LA, he was fascinated. By the end of the flight, he had given me three different private numbers for him, and also his mother's number. You're not a true celebrity unless you have more cellphones than hands.

"I like the way you think," he told me. He said he wanted to have me talk to his mother, Dr. Donda West. He thought because of our mutual interest in faith and our humanitarian work, we would get along. Two days later I called his mother. She was a classy, highly educated woman—she had been an English professor for decades and during her career had run the English departments at two universities, Clark Atlanta and Chicago State. She had retired from academia to help manage the phenomenon that was her son.

Over the next couple of weeks, I spent many hours with Kanye, often while he was in the studio working on his next album, which turned out to be the Grammy Award–winning *Graduation*. While we talked, I watched him build the song "Stronger" literally from beginning to end. It was fascinating to watch a young genius at work. I spent time with Donda in the studio while he created. We talked about important work we might do together. She seemed to really like me being around Kanye.

I think more than any other person in our lives, mothers are in touch with supernatural signals often without even recognizing it. They seem to walk around with a Miracle Mentality when it comes to their kids. How many mothers out there get a message from somewhere on high when their children are in trouble? For those of us who aren't mothers, how often do we call our moms or walk into her presence and she instantly knows exactly what we've been going through, like she's been reading our emails and text messages? It happens to me all the time. I'll walk into my mom's place and she'll tell me, "Tim, you need to get some rest." I'll have a shocked reaction, trying to convince her otherwise.

"No, Mom, I look good!"

She'll shrug, unconvinced. "Yeah, you look good. But you need to slow down and get some rest."

My mouth will hit the floor because I'll know she's exactly right—she's nailed precisely what's going on with me.

Our mothers usually don't stop with identifying the problem. They also pray for us and are open to what God is telling them. They're communing with God, asking him to guard us, protect us, help us work through our obstacles. That was what Dr. West was doing in Kanye's life, trying to connect with her supernatural powers to help watch over him.

I was so shocked and disturbed when I got the news in November 2007 that this lovely woman was gone. Right away my thoughts went to Kanye. Without his mother around to help protect and watch over him, I knew he'd be facing some difficult times ahead.

Messy to Magical

The first and most important step in moving from messy to magical as a parent is to *wake up,* just like Laurence Fishburne's character screams in the Spike Lee film *School Daze.* You have to realize if you are raising your children amid a chaotic state that it will ultimately have a major impact on their development.

Once you have committed yourself to making changes, you must *take inventory.* That means you look at every aspect of your parenting and determine the areas you sense are less than ideal for optimal development of your child(ren). For the family down the street from me, whom I will call the Parkers, taking inventory meant Mr. and Mrs. Parker had to wake up one morning, look around, and realize that having dog crap all over the floors of their house was not acceptable and reclining on the couch in a layer of dog hair was nasty.

After you take an honest inventory of your life and the state of mess it is in, you must *create an action plan.* This is perhaps the most important step. It's not enough to recognize the clutter and chaos without deciding how you will eliminate it. What change is going to bring about the transformation you need? How are you going to get from A to B?

In crafting your plan, the best way to accomplish your goals is to get some assistance from an *accountability partner.* I do a lot of work with people recovering from addiction. I am the co-owner of five rehabilitation centers because I think it's such important work. I'm inside a rehab center every single week of my life, at least two days a week. A major element of addiction recovery is relying on an accountability partner to keep you honest during the rough patches that are surely going to come.

In the case of the Parkers, my neighbors down the street, they needed friends who were going to be brutally honest with them. "Hey, I love you guys, but the last few times I've come here you've seemed overwhelmed. Do you need any help? We can hire someone to help you clean the place if that's proving to be a challenge for you."

Nothing too severe or offensive. Maybe they hadn't even realized how overwhelmed they were. Or maybe the parents came from childhoods where their parents were messy. Had someone confronted them, it would have been their chance to reverse the curse.

The wealthy businessman whose family was spiraling out of

control had been awakened to the problem and he had taken inventory. He knew things had gotten bad while he was off making money. Now he was ready for an action.

I told him, "Hey, unfortunately you're going to have to put the work trips on hold. Even if the result is that you make less money, we've got to stop the bleeding." He agreed. He realized it was time to trust his employees to do their jobs and take up the slack. They stepped up and did stellar work in his absence. But when he delved into his family's problems, he reported to me that things were worse than he had known. His child's addiction was more severe than he suspected, and she was spending time with characters he considered unsavory. Then she got pregnant by somebody she hardly knew. He had not been guarding or governing his family.

I sometimes talk in sermons about the importance of a soldier guarding their post in the military. All the branches of the military have general orders that apply to anyone assigned sentry duty. Chief among the orders is this one: "I will guard everything within the limits of my post and quit my post only when properly relieved." The last part is especially essential—you don't stop guard duty until you are assured that someone else has relieved you. This should be taken to heart by every parent watching over their offspring.

The same concept applies in sports. In a zone defense in basketball, your responsibility is to cover an area. If you move outside of your area to try to make a steal or because of a lack of discipline, the defense will break down and present the other team with holes they can exploit. In football, the defender assigned to cover the corner has to remain on the corner, no matter what he thinks is going to happen with the offensive play. If you watch a game and see the defender on the end overcommit to the inside, a speedy runner will fly past him around the corner and usually get a big gain.

The point can't be emphasized enough: when you have children, you must protect and watch over them at all times. This can be tough when you're not living in the same household as the child. Figuring out how to guide, guard, and govern can get complicated—particularly if you're getting resistance from the other parent. When I got divorced, it was very painful for me to figure out how to go from being around my son and daughter all the time to becoming this guy who came to pick them up to bring them places. Divorce had turned my ex and me into a "divided force." I felt like I had become Disneyland Dad, something with which I'm sure many divorced dads can identify. The memories still pain me.

On more than one occasion I'd come knock on the door and my ex wouldn't even answer it; she'd leave me standing outside the door, feeling like an idiot. I'd call and she wouldn't answer the phone. Finally, after I knocked and knocked for a while, she'd open the door with barely a greeting. In the first months after the divorce, sometimes she wouldn't open the door at all. Anything she could do to get under my skin.

When the children would come out, I'd have to brush away my extreme irritation and put on my happy face. Everything would be over-the-top fake excitement. That worked for a while, but as they got older and more sophisticated, they began to pick up on the fakeness.

One time when I picked them up, I said, "Okay, guys, listen, we did Disneyland last week. This time let's go to Downtown Disney. They got this restaurant I want to try." I turned to my daughter. "Then I'll take you to Sephora," I said, giving her my fully animated voice.

My daughter was about twelve at the time. She looked at me closely.

"Dad, it doesn't always have to be an event or an occasion," she said. "Let's just go to your house."

That blew me away. I realized the important thing was us spending time together, not trying to come up with once-in-a-lifetime experiences every single weekend. Children are much more intuitive than we give them credit for, especially in reading their parents. In effect, this is when they develop their emotional intelligence, discerning their parents' moods.

Children also become adept at picking up on people who have a magical aura around them, people who have the Miracle Mentality in abundance. I believe when you live the magical lifestyle, you become like a walking billboard that people can read and sense. Do you remember when your children were little and there were certain adults they seemed to like instantly and others they shied away from? They were being drawn in by the ones who had the Miracle Mentality, whose lives were filled with magic.

But it's difficult to talk about magical living when you're in a messy place. You're just trying to survive; you're not really thinking about thriving. Often you're holding on for dear life. I recently shared the stage at a large Las Vegas convention with Kevin Hart and Floyd Mayweather where they talked about their childhoods. Though their careers were radically different, a comedian/movie star and a championship boxer, the stories of their early lives were remarkably similar. Both of them were raised in the mess, in families that had severe financial struggles and were in a constant state of disarray. Both men said living in that mountain of mess triggered something in them: a vow that they would become the answer to the family's struggles. In the face of the mess some people get intimidated and cower. Some get frustrated and freeze. But some get motivated and tell themselves, *I'm going to change this crap. I will reverse the curse.* That's exactly what both of these men did.

Mad

How do we identify madness? How do people know when they're in a state of madness as parents?

You have lost your direction. Peace and rest are lacking in your life. You have a difficult time getting to sleep at night because you are stewing inside a vat of bedlam. You experience a paucity of hope; you've become so overwhelmed you want to give up.

If you are a parent and you and your family are experiencing conditions like this, you have lost control. You are no longer guiding, guarding, and governing your children because you likely aren't doing those things for your own life. The children are left to their own devices, essentially raising themselves—with often-disastrous results. When researchers at Seattle's Center for Integrative Brain Research subjected baby mice to a constant stream of stimulation—extreme audio and visual stimulation for six hours a day for several weeks—the mice later showed severe effects such as hyperactivity, increased risk-taking, diminished short-term memory, and decreased cognitive function.[3] It's not hard to see how this experiment applies to children raised amid madness, receiving an overabundance of stimuli.

Over the years I have had the opportunity to get to know music legend Quincy Jones extremely well as a friend and a client. I can't imagine anyone having a childhood more immersed in madness than his. Although he has had one of the most incredible careers in entertainment history, he has spent most of his adult life dealing with the remnants of childhood trauma. When Quincy was just seven, he watched his mother descend into insanity. Sarah Jones was a beautiful, college-educated woman who spoke several languages and had the respect of everyone in their Chicago neighborhood. But her hold on reality began to slip in Quincy's early years—to the point where Quincy's father, Quincy Sr., had her taken away in a straitjacket and delivered to a mental hospital. Little Quincy had a close-up view of the entire drama.

When he was nine and his brother, Lloyd, was seven, their father couldn't handle the child-rearing on his own and brought them to their grandmother in Louisville. But their grandmother, a proud woman who was born into slavery, was poor. So poor that Quincy and Lloyd often were sent down to the Ohio River to hunt rats for dinner.

"She told us that the more the rats wiggle their tails, the better they'd taste," Quincy wrote in his astounding memoir, *Q: The Autobiography of Quincy Jones.* "So we'd wait by the river, snatch up the biggest ones we could find by the tail, and stuff them in a burlap sack."[4]

If you have doubt whether hunting for the most edible rats is traumatic, join me for a moment and conjure a mental image of the last rat you saw. Zoom in and picture the pointy little face, the beady eyes, maybe even the high-pitched squeals they sometimes make. Do you have the image fixed in your mind? Okay, now take a bite.

That kind of hunger was traumatic enough, but what happened after they went back to live with their father in Chicago made my head nearly explode the first time I heard the story. Quincy and Lloyd ached for their missing mother as they watched their father unsuccessfully try to manage raising them alone. One day their father loaded them into his car and announced that they were going to visit their mother.

"Fear raced through my insides as the engine roared to life," Quincy wrote. "I loved my mother, but I didn't know who she was and I feared her. I feared the pain she wrought on my soul and hers. I feared the confusion, that feeling that maybe I did something that made her sick, or that maybe Daddy did it, or maybe Lloyd did it, who knew?"[5]

When they got to the mental hospital in Kankakee, Illinois, they encountered the manic, angry, ghost-like presence of Sarah Jones, who loudly ranted at the three of them. Quincy Sr. kept imploring her to say hello to her sons, but she refused.

"She gestured angrily and began to yell louder, almost hysterically, then suddenly stopped short and froze," Quincy wrote. "Her waving arms grew still, and in what seemed to be a cone of silence, she squatted on her haunches. She placed her hands behind her knees, defecated into one palm, drew the hand out from beneath her, then dipped a finger into her own feces, using it as a fork. She then raised the finger full of shit to her mouth."

An enraged Quincy Sr. was able to knock the feces out of her hands before she ate it. But the damage was done. The madness had settled deep into their souls.

"We were starving, for food, for affection, for love," Quincy's brother, Lloyd, said in the book. "We didn't know nothing about that. I read once that a child needs twelve hugs a day to be successful in life. Me and Quincy didn't get twelve hugs in twenty years."

Developmental psychologists like Sigmund Freud and Erik Erikson would have had many years' worth of material studying the effects of such outrageous events on Quincy's young psyche. When I began to have long talks with him, we spent many hours discussing the pain he still carried from his childhood. He was grappling with questions about whether God was truly there for him as he was growing up. He had lived for more than eighty years, had survived two brain aneurysms, had seen the failure of multiple marriages, and was trying to keep all the moving pieces of his life and family together. Looking at his brilliant work, at the riches he had accrued, at the abundance of love that surrounded, it was clear that he had seen magic throughout his adult life. But he didn't always feel it.

Mad to Magical

In building a path from mad to magical, I turn first to the wonder of Psalm 23. One of the best-known and frequently referenced sections of the Bible, Psalm 23 has brought comfort and answers to many people over the generations.

> The LORD is my shepherd; I shall not want.
> He maketh me to lie down in green pastures: he leadeth me
>   beside the still waters.
> He restoreth my soul: he leadeth me in the paths of
>   righteousness for his name's sake.
> Yea, though I walk through the valley of the shadow of death,
>   I will fear no evil: for thou art with me; thy rod and thy
>   staff they comfort me.
> Thou preparest a table before me in the presence of mine
>   enemies: thou anointest my head with oil; my cup
>   runneth over.
> Surely goodness and mercy shall follow me all the days of my
>   life: and I will dwell in the house of the LORD for ever.

You can try looking inside to get out of the madness, but sometimes you are just not strong enough. Psalm 23 can be a huge help to you. It says that the Lord, as your shepherd, guides you, guards you, and governs you. That's what a shepherd is. "I shall not want" means that you shall not have anxious desires. That is the power of the Lord in our lives. He will save you from the anxious desires that come with madness.

In my research I came upon an intriguing discovery about the nature of sheep. If a sheep has been challenged in the past by a predator, that sheep has a difficult time resting. But as long as the sheep can see the shepherd, the sheep is peaceful. That is the power of the Lord in our lives.

Verse 2, "He maketh me to lie down in green pastures," implies that knowing God is your shepherd can make you feel good enough, comfortable enough, to lie down in green pastures. You can rest because he restores your soul, and when your soul is restored, you find peace.

While I believe the comfort you can find in Psalm 23 can help you discover your path out of madness, there are also other ways you can bring shepherds into your life—living representations of the Lord whose presence gives you comfort and hope. When I was a young minister traveling around the country, I met a woman named Fay who told me she was a big fan of mine and invited me to her house. When I walked into this eighty-two-year-old woman's home I was swept away by the tranquility and divinity I felt in that space. I actually came up with an excuse so that I could stay there longer than planned. She was so centered, so full of grace, that I asked her, "Fay, why is there so much peace in this house?"

"Tim, I don't watch that much TV," she said. "I don't listen to a lot of crazy music. I just have really good prayer times here."

She had turned her home into a sanctuary of God. We can re-create that in our homes, for our families. Doing that becomes absolutely necessary if we are going to find a way out of madness. We have to turn our physical spaces into powerful places that can be an oasis for us and our children. We also need to surround ourselves with people who can bring us peace because they have that kind of impact on our souls. Whether we find them in church or in the house down the street, we have to figure out how to have those sorts of people in our lives.

I have often been told that I can have a calming, centering effect on people. One day a few years back I got an interesting message from my assistant. She laid out for me a remarkable situation that was transpiring in Michigan. A man there had been in a serious accident that had put him in a coma, but he had recently woken up. The man's family told my assistant that his seven-year-old son kept insisting that the family call me to come pray for him.

"Are you going to be in Michigan any time soon?" asked my sister, who was at my house.

"You know, I actually *will* be in Michigan in a few days," I said. "The hospital is just forty-five minutes from where I'm going to speak."

When I got to the hospital four days later, I was greeted by a large group of the man's friends and family, at least fifteen people. A little kid excitedly raced up to hug me.

"Mommy, Tim Storey's here! It's gonna be okay!"

The mother explained to me that her son had seen me speak at their church months earlier on a Sunday morning. He begged them to return to hear me again on Monday, when I preached again. He saw me heal many people in the church, moving in miracles. When his dad had the accident, hurtling the family into a state of madness, the kid immediately had a solution: call Tim Storey. That was a child with a firm grasp on the Miracle Mentality.

Because of that child's intervention, I was able to bring a much-needed dose of hope to that family. In the boy's mind, I had some sort of superpowers. But in reality, I was just a man who cared and made the decision to show up for them. Family members told me afterward that the family's demeanor changed when I got there and talked to them. I could feel that their hope was diminishing. I told them that I didn't believe his time was up, that he had a lot more to accomplish, and we had to believe God was going to finish what he'd started in this man's life. It was an emotional scene, with lots of tears in the room.

The little boy sat right next to me the whole time, watching my every move. His father made it through the ordeal. He stayed in touch with me for years afterward, always telling me how thankful he was. But it all began with the child leading the way.

CHAPTER 5

Love Relationships

Our love relationship is probably the most important relationship most of us will have in our lives. As a matter of fact, I would say the health of our relationships, in parenting, with our partner, and in our friendships (the subject of the next chapter), is the most critical factor in assessing how we feel about our lives. Of course, the topics in the rest of the book—career, finances, and health—are extremely important as well, but in terms of our day-to-day mindset and the level of life satisfaction, I think we can accurately predict someone's state of mind by assessing their parenting, love, and friendship relationships.

I'm sure most of us have noticed that when we are in the midst of a powerful love affair, the sun just seems to shine brighter. The other aspects of our lives seem to be proceeding on a more positive track, we are happier, and we have a much sunnier outlook on how each day will go. People glow when they're in love. I think when we're experiencing a victory as major as a successful love relationship, we develop faith that we will have victories in other areas. We start looking to win. Studies have even shown that happily married people enjoy better overall health than those who are unhappily married.[1]

When the love relationship is not going well, a long list of negative effects follows. One study found that people who are experiencing marital conflict and depression have a higher incidence of poor digestive health.[2] Another study revealed that strained relationships may be connected to increased risk for heart disease.[3] When you have a loss in your marriage, that big *L* is so powerful and all-consuming that it makes you start looking around, waiting to see what other disasters are going to befall you. You start seeing your life through the lens of the loss.

Mundane in Love

Relationship pain is all around us; I've experienced quite a bit of it myself. I think about this issue all the time—oddly enough, particularly when I'm stuck in traffic. Even if you don't live with me here in Southern California, you've probably heard about our traffic. It's a sadistic daily experiment in human torture; only those with steely nerves and vast reserves of patience can emerge with their sanity intact. Los Angeles County has more cars in it than any other county in America, right around twelve million of them. Every driver in Los Angeles experiences a whopping 119 hours of delays on average every year.[4] That's more than two full days spent in delayed traffic each year, and nine hours more than any other city in America.

But a corollary to our traffic nightmare is that while sitting in our air-conditioned cars, literally cooling our heels, we all are unwilling receptacles of that necessary oil in the capitalist engine: advertising. No matter how much you try to find tools of distraction, you can't help but notice the billboards that line the freeways like skid row panhandlers.

What are these billboards telling us? Ultimately, in dozens of ways, that we have to be better, be perfect. This one is screaming at us that we need liposuction. That one is pushing veneers for our teeth. Over here we're being implored to pay a surgeon to take off thirty years from our face. Over there we're being sold on a radical new diet. And finally, the divorce lawyers are telling us they're ready to clean up the mess we cause when we fail to be perfect for our significant others.

Yes, our love relationships are often the unwitting victims of the incessant sensory overload that is life in modern America. Sometimes it feels nearly impossible to keep the fires alive and another human being happy with themselves and with us when we are all being told we're not good enough. But despite the seeming impossibility of nurturing successful relationships, we still expect them to fulfill all our needs—and inevitably feel the inescapable drag of failure when they don't. We know the divorce rate in the United States sits somewhere between 40 and 50 percent, meaning a great many of these couplings that start with such boundless promise will one day collapse. But it's hard not to be shocked by personal failure and internalize the disappointment when it all comes crashing down—particularly when there are kids involved. That's certainly what happened to me when my marriage ended in 1999.

After experiencing a childhood that was disturbing in many ways, as I discussed earlier, I thought I had stepped into family nirvana when I married Cindy Miranda. Her father, Jesse Miranda, was an esteemed religious leader in the Latin community, a man with more degrees than I had shoes. Her mother, who oozed style and class, was an accomplished person in her own right, the head of the trauma department at a famous hospital. When I looked at her,

I immediately thought of the elegant Mexican artist Frida Kahlo. Cindy, who was a senior at University of Southern California when we got together, was also an exceptional woman of class and beauty. I used to love walking into their home and feeling enveloped by the peace and serenity of the place.

But, alas, I don't think I was equipped to handle what I was being given in the marriage, probably because of my past. I had charisma, I had humor, I had good intentions, but I did not have the right tools and skills to be a good spouse. I think a lot of us enter relationships with the same failings—namely, a background during which we were not given the tools we would need to thrive.

One of the fateful decisions I made, at least in terms of the preservation of my marriage, was starting the Hollywood Bible Study. Though I brought together an incredibly diverse collection of entertainers and power brokers to offer one another spiritual sustenance, my wife hated it. She didn't like the Hollywood glitz of it all. In the five years I led the Bible study, between 1992 and 1997, Cindy came to the gathering a total of two times. I began to feel like there was an ever-widening chasm between my two worlds that I could not close. This was when my mundane began to look a lot more like frustration.

Even worse, she started to fill the heads of my son and daughter with the idea that I had "gone big-time" and was no longer the same person. I remember one outing with my son that exemplified how bad the situation had become.

Dyan Cannon had offered me her seats to the Lakers, which happened to be courtside. I excitedly told my eleven-year-old son all about it.

"Nah, I'm not into it," he said in response.

I was shocked. "Are you joking? We'd be sitting right next to Magic Johnson!" I said.

But he persisted, still shaking his head. I couldn't believe it.

About a year later when she offered the tickets again, he agreed to go with me. As advertised, the seats were amazing. We *were* sitting next to Magic, and next to him was the guy who started Guess jeans, and next to him was the talented comedic actor Jim Carrey. This was during the height of Carrey's powers—he had just made movies like *Ace Ventura* and *Liar Liar*. Next to Carrey was Tiger Woods, who had just won the Masters for the first time. My son spent quite a bit of time talking to the Guess jeans guy. After the game, I was eager to have him tell me how giddy he was about it all.

"Do you know who you were talking to? The guy who started Guess jeans!" I said. "And did you see Carrey and Tiger?"

"Yeah," he said, totally lacking emotion. This was not my kid, not the ebullient little guy I knew and loved.

I frowned. "How come you aren't excited?" I asked.

He turned to me and said, "Dad, because that's not what life is about."

I was floored. His lips were moving, but I knew the words were his mother's.

I had a difficult time coping with the end of the marriage. She told me that I wasn't there for her emotionally, that I didn't listen to her. I think to a certain extent she was right. I poured so much of myself into my job, into helping other people, that I had little left by the time I got to her. I think a lot of hardworking men find themselves getting hit by the same accusations. I was still funny when I got home, I was still trying to please her, I was still taking out the trash and doing my husbandly duties, but she always seemed to be pissed at me.

When it was over, I started drinking for the first time, maybe a couple times a week. I didn't get drunk, and I didn't develop a craving for it. But I liked how soothing having a glass of bourbon in the evenings was. I was losing my way, looking in the wrong places for solace—turning to temporary vices rather than the healing power of God. I also started spending more time with guys like Charlie Sheen, Robert Downey Jr., Darryl Strawberry, and a bunch of NFL players. I think I liked being with those guys because they were dealing with stuff that made me feel like the crap I was struggling with wasn't so bad after all.

Deep down inside I knew I couldn't go on like this. I needed help. I had to find my center again, recalibrate my satellite dish. A friend told me about a therapist in downtown Los Angeles who he thought could work magic with a guy like me. Wow, was he right. But I sure didn't make it easy for the talented Dr. M. When I first parked my car in downtown Los Angeles and strode into her office, I was as eager to be there as if I were about to have a double root canal. After all, I counseled others for a living. What could this woman do for me? And more importantly, how much would she be expecting me to reveal about myself? In other words, I came to her with the opposite of the Miracle Mentality.

Wearing my swag on my sleeve, I walked into her office, looked around, and proceeded to ask her if I could sit in the fancy chair. The one with her sweater hanging off the back. I knew the chair facing the couch was not the one designed for the patient, but I asked her anyway.

"Don't you think that looks like my seat?" she asked.

"Why?" I said.

"'Cause my sweater's right there," she said calmly.

Dr. M figured me out quickly. I was entitled and I didn't even realize it. I was caught up in the trappings of my success. But she had some powerful lessons in store for me. By the third session, she was digging deep, asking me what I was covering up.

"Why are you coming to counseling but talking to me in sound bites, telling me what you think I want to hear?"

She made me realize I had been walking around for twenty years with what she called an "orphan's heart." I was a nice guy just looking to fit in somewhere, likely because of the losses I endured during my childhood. But I wasn't going to let anybody into my head or my heart. Her words shook me to my core. I thought back to all the years of hearing girlfriends and my wife tell me they couldn't understand why they couldn't connect with me.

One of the first realizations I had after my marriage went south was that I had stopped trying to connect with my wife. This is extremely common in our love relationships; we seem to forget about doing all the things that brought us together and made us click in the beginning. Remember what you did when you first started dating your significant other, all the extra steps you took to make everything perfect? You were hit by those pheromones and felt like you were on the set of a Hollywood rom-com, playing Matthew McConaughey's or Sandra Bullock's part. Everything was filled with magic. You put deep thought into the song you would play on the car stereo when you picked her up for those early dates. It was time for some love music—Luther Vandross, Maxwell, Sade. What about the restaurant? Oh man, that required hours of research. And then a walk on the beach under the moonlight. Or a stroll in Central Park. Yeah, you were intent on creating magic.

But then you stopped. The magic worked; you're together now. So you get comfortable. The planning goes out the window. You aren't trying to connect with each other anymore. The two of you engage in this endless and painfully mundane debate about where you will go for dinner on date night. I was talking to one couple about their routine and the husband proudly told me they never missed a date night. The wife looked at me and rolled her eyes.

"Yeah, it's always so exciting," she said, but he didn't even pick up on the sarcasm.

He's checking date night off his list every week so he thinks he's done his duty. But weekly date night dinner isn't nearly enough. That is the epitome of mundane. It'd be like giving your child the same birthday party every year; a twelve-year-old isn't likely to be feeling Chuck E. Cheese. I saw all kinds of danger signs flashing on the horizon for that couple. There's no overestimating how much effort it takes to keep a relationship from slipping from magical to mundane. Relationships are not for the faint of heart. But so many things rest on our ability to keep the magic alive. In my experience, a huge percentage of American marriages are sitting uncomfortably in the mundane, on the verge of becoming a problem, becoming messy or even mad.

Mundane to Magical

From a biblical standpoint, your priorities in your family should be clear: God first, your spouse second, your kids third, your job fourth. If your spouse doesn't come after God, challenges will arise with the children. Too many people in our society skip over the spouse and go straight from God to the children; I see it every day. Some even skip the kids and go straight from God to career. And it's important for children to see the amazing role the mother and father play in the life of the family. In my life coaching, I often see families where the husband doesn't show respect for his spouse or partner, and as a result, the children think they don't need to show the spouse or partner respect. Needless to say, that is not a formula for magic.

Once the initial love connection is made, it is incumbent on both parties to make sure the fire stays hot, to remain connected, to cultivate the relationship. That means plow the ground, plant the seed, water the seed, and reap the bounty of the harvest. *Connect* and *cultivate*. Cultivation in the context of a love relationship is all about quality time, quality conversations, quality intimacy. I think we all know the difference between quality and quantity. Quality is the stuff you did in the beginning when you were creating magic. Quality intimacy isn't just about sex either. It could mean lying on the couch together watching a good movie or holding hands while you walk in the park. Because we typically started our relationships in a magical state, I think most people instinctively know what steps would need to be taken to get back there, but they are just too lazy to make the effort.

In addition to *connect* and *cultivate*, I am adding a third C: *create*. You must go out of your way in love relationships to create opportunities for magical moments. I watched a recent episode of the reality show *The Bachelor* and noted how the producers set up the last four dates the guy went on with his prospective brides. The prior dates had been good dates, fun dates, but at the end it was time to create the real magic. He went on a helicopter tour with one woman. Another he took out to sea on a sailboat. Each date got progressively more amazing.

The lesson? The effort is extremely important. We need to regularly take *inventory* of how much effort we are putting into creating magic in our love relationships. Are you putting your spouse second, before the kids—and after God?

In my coaching I frequently run into the question of blame: Who's at fault when the magic is gone? Is it just the husband's job to keep the fires hot? Is it fair for the wife to wait for him to initiate everything?

The finger-pointing, the blame game, all of that has to stop. It's not productive, it benefits no one, and it drains energy that could have been directed elsewhere. In the end, it's a job husband and wife share, just as they are supposed to be partners in the child-rearing. In order to share any job, communication is crucial. No relationship book written doesn't highlight the word *communication* at some point in the text. When you sense that the magic has drained away, you have to talk about it. During those talks, you must be honest about what you think you're missing. Once you get to that point, I love the next thing you must do: *take action steps*.

The list of fun activities you can undertake together is endless, ranging from tennis or bowling to gardening or jigsaw puzzles. The thing you do isn't as important as the time you spend together. Be creative. You can even do chores together—spring cleaning, purging junk from the garage, holding a yard sale. You can exercise together or just go on regular walks. These little things can make big differences. And whatever you do, put your phone away!

I am reminded of a couple I was coaching. The lady kept complaining the man was too busy, and they had not taken a quality vacation in a couple of years.

"Tim, I would like to plan at least two quality vacations a year," she told me.

I said that was a fair request. They were a wealthy couple—he owned a successful business—so money wasn't a problem. The three of us put our heads together and came up with two quality vacations—a cruise and a trip to Hawaii—plus a shorter weekend getaway to the wine country in Sonoma. But she insisted on one rule: he could only be on his phone for two hours a day. He agreed; he said he would get on the phone for an hour early in the day to check on his employees, then at the end of the day he would check in to make sure everything was okay.

I was ecstatic at the report I got when they came back. The trips really lit a fire in their marriage.

She said to me, "Tim, I've never had that much time alone with him in twelve years."

In private he told me, "Man, I wish I would have done this a long time ago. My mind has not been this clear in a long time."

The experience gave him the bonus of finding out he could trust his employees to hold the company down; he had trained them well. This meant he could devote even more time to his wife going forward. That was three years ago, and I still help them decide where they are going every year. It's a source of great excitement for both of them. This was a couple on the verge of filing for divorce; now they're happier than ever. They have a firm grasp of the Miracle Mentality.

When we are in the middle of a failing relationship, our minds get clouded with so much noise in the form of jealousy, hostility, and insecurity that it becomes nearly impossible to get back to the things that are important to our lives.

Messy

At some point, messy tries to invade every relationship. It must be one of the laws of physics or something. A messy relationship feels disheveled, disorderly—it starts to lose its rhythm. It can begin with something as simple as you no longer sending little love texts to your partner during the course of the day. You're getting increasingly busy at work and you just don't have the time. And it seemed like she didn't really care that much anyway.

You stop leaving notes for each other around the house like you used to in the beginning. You would slip a sexy note inside of his briefcase before he left for work. But you're so rushed getting the kids off to school in the morning, who has time for all that?

You keep forgetting that Wednesday is trash day. You're so busy with major projects that you have to bring your work home with you and you just don't have the bandwidth to stay on top of the trash pickup schedule. You can just bring it down to the town dump yourself anyway, no big deal. But you can't seem to find the time to make that trip, so the trash piles up in the garage, even though your wife keeps asking you to take care of it.

You used to dress so sharp when you went out on date nights with your spouse, but your attire has gotten increasingly messy and casual over the last couple of years. Hey, you have to dress up for work; why should you do it again just to go to the same restaurants you always go to?

The last time you stepped on the scale, the numbers told you that you were twenty pounds heavier than you were a few years ago. With all the kids' practices and the overtime at work, it's been really hard to get in the workouts you used to do. And how are you going to turn down all those free corporate lunches, no matter how high the calorie content?

The thread that runs through all these examples is that you were putting other things before your spouse and your relationship, moving your significant other lower and lower on your list of priorities. What may have started as mundane has now become a mess—and it's starting to show in how you two are getting along. You're fighting more frequently, spending more time away from each other, having less sex. You've become too comfortable in the comfortable.

Let me give you an example from an experience I had a few years back in Spain. I was eating lunch with a sharp, good-looking couple whose company I enjoyed. The conversation was engaging, the food delectable, the weather perfect as we sat in an outdoor café. It was like a scene lifted from a tourist brochure. In the midst of the witty repartee, the unmistakable sound of a fart broke through the conversation like an exploding bomb.

"Oh my God!" the woman said as she looked at her boyfriend in horror.

"Come on, babe," he said with a grin. "You've heard it before."

I looked at him. I wasn't grinning. "Oh man, you did that on purpose?"

"Yeah. It's not good to hold it."

"Oh man," I said again, frowning. "That's just not right."

The conversation continued for a while longer, but I couldn't get over what had happened. I've never been one to pass gas in front of my woman; it seems the epitome of rude and disrespectful to me. But that's how the mess starts to creep in. You relax your standards, lower the bar little by little for how much respect and consideration you give your partner.

This state recalls similarities with the broken windows theory of policing Rudy Giuliani championed when he was mayor of New York City. First introduced to the public in a 1982 article in the *Atlantic Monthly* by social scientists James Q. Wilson and George L. Kelling, the theory is that policing practices that focus on minor crimes, like vandalism, public drinking, and fare evasion, create an atmosphere of order and respect for the law, which subsequently stops people from committing more serious crimes.

The authors wrote,

Social psychologists and police officers tend to agree that if a window in a building is broken and is left unrepaired, all the rest of the windows will soon be broken. This is as true in nice neighborhoods as in rundown ones. Window-breaking does not necessarily occur on a large scale because some areas are inhabited by determined window-breakers whereas others are populated by window-lovers; rather, one unrepaired broken window is a signal that no one cares, and so breaking more windows costs nothing.[5]

The authors' belief is that if you address problems when they are small, such as repairing a broken window within a day or cleaning the sidewalk every day, wrongdoers will be less likely to break more windows or to litter. Though the theory has been consistently attacked because many believe it led to New York's controversial "stop-and-frisk" policy—which sent millions of black and brown men to jail and was subsequently ruled unconstitutional—it's easy to see how it can apply to relationships. When you let things start slipping in a partnership, you open the door to more serious relationship offenses.

In my experience, the messes begin to manifest in many ways—someone forgets their partner's birthday, an important anniversary is ignored, one partner forgets an event that had been planned for months. In addition to forgetting, both sides start reneging on promises. You were supposed to take a much-needed vacation in August, but your spouse bows out at the last minute because something important came up at work—once again putting other things ahead of the relationship. And showing a decided lack of remorse about it.

"Oh, I'm sure you understand. I'm just so busy."

Messy will soon descend into arguments, anger, and resentment if it's not addressed. Once you get there, the trip from messy to mad is dangerously short.

Mad

Remember how hard it was to concentrate at work the last time you were going through major stress in your life? That's when you know your relationship has descended into madness—you can't ever seem to focus because your thoughts keep going back to home. You lose your sense of contentment, which is one of the most important aspects of a successful relationship. You know you're in the madness when you are no longer at peace. I go to my rock for assistance here, the Bible—specifically Galatians 5:

> This I say then, Walk in the Spirit, and ye shall not fulfil the lust of the flesh. For the flesh lusteth against the Spirit, and the Spirit against the flesh: and these are contrary the one to the other: so that ye cannot do the things that ye would. But if ye be led of the Spirit, ye are not under the law. Now the works of the flesh are manifest, which are these; Adultery, fornication, uncleanness, lasciviousness, idolatry, witchcraft, hatred, variance, emulations, wrath, strife, seditions, heresies, envyings, murders, drunkenness, revellings, and such like: of the which I tell you before, as I have also told you in time past, that they which do such things shall not inherit the kingdom of God. But the fruit of the Spirit is love, joy, peace, longsuffering, gentleness, goodness, faith, meekness, temperance: against such there is no law. And they that are Christ's have crucified the flesh with the affections and lusts. If we live in the Spirit, let us also walk in the Spirit. Let us not be desirous of vain glory, provoking one another, envying one another. (vv. 16–26)

When you're in the madness, you're walking in the works of the flesh, not in the fruit of the Spirit.

How can you tell the difference between the messy and the mad in your love relationship? A big difference is that in the messy, you're not being distracted from your day-to-day life. You're still talking to each other; you're still maybe going on the occasional date night;

you're still sharing household responsibilities; you may still be having regular sex. In the madness, these things are not typically on the schedule anymore. Too much resentment and hostility have built up to conduct these regular relationship activities. You're depleted, distracted, and devastated. Bad things start happening, such as infidelity and big-time disrespect. One or both of you become dramatic in the midst of the drama. What I mean is, you start making choices you would not usually make. When you're in the right state of mind and drama hits, most people don't react with more drama. But in the madness you do crazy stuff—throw things, break stuff, storm out of rooms with doors slammed, yell at the kids, even pull a Bernadine Harris and make a bonfire with your partner's clothes.

While my own marriage never got to the point of bonfires, we definitely were sliding from the messy into the mad in the end. Through my own failures I've learned the importance of repairing these relationship problems—in addition to years of work with therapists and marriage counselors and my own clients. My ex and I went from the mundane to the messy, then started to trickle into madness before we called it quits. Disagreements that used to be settled amicably escalated into arguments. Our perspectives on how we should raise our two children began to drastically diverge. But because my ex was not the type who wanted to hash things out, conflict would inevitably be followed by the serious silent treatment. That's how she showed me her displeasure. Crickets. I knew things were getting bad and would often try to get into a conversation with her, but she wouldn't engage. It was a particularly painful retaliation for me, someone who enjoys talking. I feel like I can say with confidence that no problem or disagreement has ever been solved with the silent treatment. If that's your preferred form of displaying your anger, realize it's going to always stand in the way of finding the magic in your relationship.

Messy and Mad to Magical

To get out of madness, you are going to need help. Rarely can a couple emerge from this on their own.

These are my action steps:

1. Reach out to God. You might find solace in Psalm 46:1–3:

> God is our refuge and strength, a very present help in trouble.
> Therefore will not we fear, though the earth be removed, and
>> though the mountains be carried into the midst of the sea;
> Though the waters thereof roar and be troubled, though the
>> mountains shake with the swelling thereof.

In times of trouble, you need to know that God is your refuge and strength. By getting closer to him, you will move closer to a place of peace in your relationship. I have seen it happen over and over again.

2. Find the correct counselor. By "correct" I mean someone who is going to understand the nature of your crisis and know how to act on it. Just because someone is really good at fixing a Mercedes doesn't mean they're going to understand a Nissan engine. You have to do some research here, ask around. I had a client recently who said his wife was unfaithful and he wanted me to recommend a counselor who could help him deal. I have about seven whom I regularly recommend to people, and while they are all good, one in particular was the right fit for him, a woman I know who does wonderful work with men in his situation.

3. Partner with the right people. If you're talking to the wrong people, you could be getting the wrong advice. That angry girlfriend whose marriage just imploded might not be the right one to share with if she's telling you to slash up all of his suits. You need to know the nature of the people around you. Can you trust them with this level of detail on your relationship? If not, don't do it.

The final point I want to make here is how to tell whether your relationship is redeemable. My answer for that is simple: *I can't answer that question for you.* That's the beautiful aspect to this—every person is different; every relationship is different; every person's tolerance is different. A horrific offense to one person might just be an annoyance to another. I met a woman in Tennessee who had recently discovered her husband was having affairs with two different women at the same time.

When I asked her how she felt about it, she said, "I need to become a better wife to him."

I was floored. *Whaaaat?* It was certainly not the answer I was expecting.

"What do you mean by that?" I asked.

"I don't believe he would have done this if I was a better wife to him," she said. "I've decided I'm going to love him so much and so well, he won't desire another woman."

As I said, the answer is different for each one of us.

CHAPTER 6

Friendships

I am often astounded by the influence our friendships have over our lives but how little attention most of us pay to them. While we usually run all kinds of parameters and possible outcomes through our minds when we're choosing a significant other, we typically don't think of any of these things when we are choosing a friend who may be around for much longer than the girlfriend or boyfriend, or even spouse. We stumble into friendships, using painfully superficial characteristics to determine whether to let someone into our circle. As adults our friendships may not begin as randomly as they did when we were kids—*That kid has a new ball; I shall play with him and he shall be my best friend*—but too often there's not a whole lot more thought applied.

I was reminded of the shallowness of friendships recently during a trip to the South. I was speaking at a church in Texarkana, Texas, a place I'd visited a number of times, and I decided to make a return visit to this amazing seafood joint called Ralph & Kacoo's, which is about ninety minutes away in Bossier City, Louisiana, right next to Shreveport. On this day a friend of mine made the drive with me, the third time I had made this drive to get that great food in a matter of months. On each trip I saw the same landscape pass by, including a scene that intrigued me: four or five black men sitting on two couches and a chair in the front yard of a house. It's the kind of scene you might see a lot in the South, where some families have an interesting idea of what constitutes lawn furniture and the weather is rarely an impediment to sitting outside. On this trip I decided to stop the car. As we got out and made our way over to the men, all sorts of thoughts were going through my head.

It's eleven in the morning. Why are they sitting on couches outside?

What are they talking about?

Why don't they have jobs? Because they all looked around forty or fifty years old.

As I approached, one of the men said, "Look at Smokey!" They all laughed. I get that all the time, people telling me I look like Smokey Robinson.

"Are you lost?" he asked me. He was clearly the ringmaster of the group. Animated, funny, fast talking—he had probably missed his calling as a comedian. Then again, he did have a captive audience of three to four guys every afternoon. And the other guys were content to let him take the lead.

"No," I said. "You guys got to help me out with something."

"What—you need directions?"

"No. I was in Texarkana because I'm speaking at a church there. I'm on my way to Shreveport to Ralph & Kacoo's."

"Oh, I love that place!" another one said. "Man, it's worth the drive."

"Yeah, I've gone there a few times," I said, "and every time I've driven by I've noticed you guys out here hanging out."

"Yeah, we're just shooting the shit," one said.

"This is interesting to me," I said. "Do you mind if I ask some questions? I'm a writer and a speaker. I could probably do a TV show on you."

"Oh man, that would be good," one of them said. "Then I wouldn't have to sit on this couch my whole life."

"Okay, so how come you guys can sit on this couch in the middle of the day? Do you work at night?"

"Well, I'm on disability," said the one who called me Smokey.

"I'm on disability too," another one said.

"I just don't feel like working right now," the third guy said.

"I'm in between," the fourth one said.

"In between what?" the first guy asked him.

"In between working and not working!"

"You never said that before," the first guy said.

"No one's ever asked," the fourth guy said.

My eyes widened. In all this time they had never discussed something as major as this guy's work situation? *Exactly how superficial were these friendships?* I wondered.

"How old are you guys?" I asked.

"I'm forty-three," one said.

I'll never forget what came next. "Damn, I didn't know that!" the second guy said.

"Why do you say it like that?" the first guy asked.

"I'm only thirty-two," the second guy said.

"No! I didn't know that!" the first guy said.

I was looking at them in shock. What in the world did they talk about?

I was fascinated that they were all clearly stuck in the same mundane place and knew so little about each other. What were they gaining from each other's company besides the comfort of another warm body? It was great that they had found one another and enjoyed spending time together, but no one in the group was living in any kind of magic or creating a spark that pushed the others. The more I dialogued with them, the more I was reminded of the old adages that misery loves company and birds of a feather flock together.

I wound up sitting with those guys for about thirty minutes, drinking a ginger ale while my companion had one of their beers. I listened to the conversation, and it was as surface as I imagined—sports, weather, local news. When we got up to leave, they were all happy about our visit and said they hoped I'd stop by again. As I got back in my car, I thought a great deal about the nature of friendships, wondering whether they would have even been able to tolerate somebody in their group who was doing well, who had a job and a healthy relationship and the drive to improve himself. That kind of a person would have presented an implicit challenge to them, making them question their own lives.

If you want to have a clear idea of which life state you're in—mundane, messy, mad, or magical—all you need do is look around and ask yourself, *What state are my friends in?*

We all have friends in our lives who serve different purposes—the party friend, the wise friend, the serious friend, the perpetually depressed friend. We often make subconscious decisions about what we need from a friend before we decide which one to call. And we know that some of our friendships would be wrecked if we tried to motivate them to lift their life out of the mundane.

A friendship is a pact, a devotion, a closeness, an agreement, an understanding. It's a relationship, a bond, a tie, an attachment. But friendships can be fraught with complications we never really want to acknowledge. Wise thinkers have pondered and written much about the nature of friendships over the years. Here are some observations that stand out to me:

"Every man becomes, to a certain degree, what the people
he generally converses with are." —Philip Dormer
Stanhope

"Surround yourself with only people who are going to lift
you higher." —Oprah Winfrey

"Associate yourself with men of good quality if you esteem
your own reputation; for 'tis better to be alone than in
bad company." —George Washington

"When I compliment you, I compliment myself, because I
am who I associate with." —Jarod Kintz

"What surrounds us is what is within us." —T. F. Hodge

"Association with other people corrupts our character;
especially when we have none." —Friedrich Nietzsche

The point is clear: you should be extremely careful when you
pick your friends.

I was amused when I came across the quote attributed to George
Washington, especially the second part of it: "'Tis better to be alone
than in bad company." All these years of hearing black women tell
each other, "I can do bad by myself"—who knew they were quoting
the father of the nation?

The people with whom we associate have a powerful ability to
influence us. That means they have the capacity to affect our behavior, our character development, our life goals, our state of mind.
Our family and friends are the most powerful influence on our lives.
As such, you must ask yourself these questions:

Are your associations lifting you up or dragging you down?

Are the people you associate with the kind of people you
would like to be?

Do your associations have the Miracle Mentality?

The Bible has something to say on this subject. For instance, Proverbs 13:20 says, "He that walketh with wise men shall be wise: but a companion of fools shall be destroyed."

In order to have a magical life, you have to have magical partnerships. I saw this lesson play out in bold relief when I was working with the actor Charlie Sheen. In the late '90s, one of Charlie's friends had started coming to my Bible study meetings, and after one of the meetings, his friend came up to me and asked if I would be willing to meet with Charlie. This was after Sheen had overdosed on cocaine so severely that he suffered a stroke and only survived after paramedics performed life-saving maneuvers when they arrived at his home. After he was forced to enter a rehab clinic, Sheen escaped and had to be returned by sheriff deputies.

Charlie asked that I come to his home, so we had a session in his Century City high-rise—me and about ten other guys sharing our stories. Charlie liked the way I dealt with him, so we began to meet every month for the next eighteen months or so. He also saw my healing work and believed in it fervently. We would get together at his place in private, and sometimes we held my Hollywood Bible Study group at his home. We would have long talks about his life, his childhood, growing up with his brother, Emilio, and his father, Martin. The idea I tried to bring to Charlie was to just get better, be better. *Not perfect. Better.* We would go through the mistakes he had made and dissect them, figure out how he had made things worse and how he was going to behave going forward. I would show him how God was there for him, guiding him in the right direction—if only he would listen and take heed.

At that time he was living a life of sobriety. But eventually he started connecting with the wrong people once again and began to make bad choices. His associates were toxic for him. He was no longer tuning in to what God was saying. He had turned away from the ways that had brought him a measure of peace. He started out approaching his problems with the desire to get better, but he reverted to the guy who was depleted and devastated, always on the brink of disaster. I hung in there with him, though it was painful to witness his relapses. I talked a lot about spirituality during our meetings, bringing him back to his biblical background. His father, Martin, a devout Catholic, was also doing the same thing, so Charlie was getting it in stereo. I was seeing a lot of growth in him. I'd bring him with me to church and chuckle to myself when people would see him in the sanctuary and do double takes. He was definitely *not* the guy most people expected to encounter on a Sunday morning. Charlie had the Miracle Mentality, but he had a difficult time holding on to it because of the environment he often found himself in and the people he surrounded himself with.

He was doing very well in the early 2000s, receiving critical acclaim and Emmy and Golden Globe award nominations for his performances in *Spin City* and then *Two and a Half Men*. For his role on *Spin City*, Sheen was reportedly paid more than any other actor on television. Charlie could be in the proper mindset, sitting comfortably with the Miracle Mentality, saying, doing, and thinking all the right things when he was with me or with his father. But then he'd be visited by someone who would shift his mindset down a dark path and his signals would get short-circuited.

In 2016, I was sitting in a restaurant at the Beverly Hills Hotel with my back to the entrance. My dinner companion said, "Hey, man, your boy just walked in." I turned around and saw that he was talking about Charlie. I hadn't seen him in two years. A Charlie sighting was rare because he preferred to spend most of his time hiding in his house. I went over and stood in front of him without saying a word. He was with a couple of his boys. He looked up and saw me.

"Aww, f**k!" he said.

"That's how you greet me?" I said.

"Damn, give me a hug!" he responded, wrapping me in a warm embrace. He turned to his bodyguard. "Didn't I tell you just two days ago that I dreamed about Tim Storey?!"

The bodyguard nodded. "For real," the bodyguard said. "Two days ago he said, 'I had a dream I was going to see Tim Storey.'"

Charlie looked at me and shook his head. "You represent the person I know I'm supposed to be. When I run into you, a flood of emotions hit me. I think about when we had it down."

Charlie repeated some of my mantras: "Don't sit in the setback. Don't settle."

"I had it down, Tim. I had it down," he said.

"Well, here I am, right now," I said. "Let's get it down again."

We spent about an hour together in the hotel restaurant, and I could tell something big was bothering him.

"I got myself into a dilemma," he said to me. "This is a big one."

Coming from Charlie's mouth, that was a little scary—this guy had been in some pretty big dilemmas in the past.

"I don't want to get into it now, but you're gonna find out. It's a big one. I'm going to need your help," he said.

"Why don't you tell me now?"

"Nah, I can't go there tonight," he said. "I got friends here. I can't go there."

I could tell the issue was too emotional for him to reveal at the moment. He thanked me for being there for him. He couldn't stop hugging me and thanking me. We exchanged private numbers, because he's always changing his number.

Charlie was right—it didn't take long for me to find out what was eating away at him. Two days later he sat on the couch of the *Today Show* and told Matt Lauer he had HIV. I felt the pain of knowing my friend was going to have challenging days ahead of him.

While Charlie's friends would get him in trouble, which is a common tale with too many celebrities, I was heartened recently when I saw the powerful images from a high-powered celebrity friendship in the making—Diddy and Jay-Z. In 2020, the video from the pre-Grammy Award brunch thrown by Roc Nation, Jay-Z's company, was beamed across social media, showing Diddy, Jay, and a bunch of other high-powered black men in snazzy suits toasting their success and black excellence surrounded by a gorgeous estate. It was the toast heard around the world. Diddy called it a "black billionaires lunch."

"You know, the game has been elevated. As far as we can tell, there's no expense being spared," Diddy said, holding aloft his champagne flute while Jay stood silently next to him in a salmon-colored suit. "And we here together and we're gonna keep staying together. United we stand and there ain't nothing else."[1]

That toast meant solidarity, these two business moguls putting aside any differences they might have had between them and forming a powerful bond. It was almost like watching friendship ascend to the top of Maslow's hierarchy—friendship self-actualization, if there is such a thing. They had achieved tremendous success in their careers, so there was no longer any possible threat between them. Game recognizing game. It was time for the love.

That toast reminded me that the Miracle Mentality can create uncommon adversaries, but in order for you to partner with power, you have to set aside any pettiness or jealousies. You have to find the common threads you share with someone who might have been an enemy or a competitor and understand how much more you can accomplish as a team as opposed to foes.

When I saw the HBO documentary on Muhammad Ali, *What's*

My Name?, I was similarly struck by the powerful friendship of Ali and Malcolm X early in Ali's career. When Malcolm was having conflict with the Honorable Elijah Muhammad, the leader of the Nation of Islam, Ali told him, "Man, you got to get it right with him. You got to get it right." In other words, we're too powerful a force together to allow quarrels to come between us.

Magical Friendships

What does magic look like in a friendship?

To answer that question, I thought back to conversations I had with Smokey Robinson about his friendship with Berry Gordy. Talk about a magic friendship! Smokey Robinson took the time to give me the history of Motown and the vision he and Berry Gordy had back in Detroit to build this historic music label. When Smokey told Berry he wanted to be more than just talent, Berry took him under his wing and taught Smokey how to be an executive and an owner. Their resulting partnership literally changed the world of music. After that conversation, I felt more magical myself. I had talked to a man who had touched the magic, had lived the magic, and now he had sprinkled some magic on me.

Magical friendships can transform your life. When you have those kinds of friends, they download the Miracle Mentality into your brain. If you have access to people in your life who already have the Miracle Mentality, do all that you can to cultivate those friendships—just as Smokey opened up to Berry.

While we know many of our friends aren't prepared to move from the mundane to the magical, by all means you should try to be a source of motivation for them. Pull as many as you can along the way as you begin to transform your life. Just don't expect everyone to follow along. You may need to let go of those who resist you—or at least temper your expectations. Call them up on occasion, have a great time with them, but protect your dreams from those who will try to destroy them out of insecurity or envy.

In the Bible, Jesus had clearly defined levels to his friendships, which I use in my coaching to teach about the power of partnerships. Of course, the highest level was the one he had with his Father. The next level was his bond with three of his disciples, Peter, James, and John, the last two known as the sons of thunder. Next was the group of twelve disciples, which included Peter, James, and John. After the twelve came the group called the seventy. And last was the multitude of five hundred.

To God, his Father, Jesus told everything. Peter, James, and John were his closest confidants, so he shared a lot with them. He told much to the disciples, but not as much as to the three. Peter, James, and John were his ride-or-dies. In the Bible when he is about to do something powerful, he takes Peter, James, and John with him while he instructs the other nine to stay back. To the seventy, Jesus mostly talks in parables, not revealing too much of his inner thoughts. To the five hundred, he only spoke in parables. A parable is defined as a rhyme or riddle. He didn't reveal everything to all of his followers because the Bible says only a fool tells his whole heart, casting their pearls before swine, which isn't the most flattering description of the multitudes. He's saying not to give your precious things to someone who doesn't value them.

When we are choosing our friends, we must remember that some people are snorkelers while others are scuba divers. The snorkelers only want to float on the surface, while the scuba divers go deep. I'm not saying you shouldn't be friends with the snorkelers—but don't expect them to do any deep diving with you, looking for magic.

CHAPTER 7

Work/Career

In my life coaching, job satisfaction is an area where I find a remarkable degree of consistency: most people aren't happy in their jobs. That's fascinating to me because I think it's such a large divergence from how we feel when we start a new job. We go in with so much hope, such high expectations. In fact, we start out with magical thinking: *Yes! This job is going to be the thing that makes me happy. It is going to fulfill my needs, utilize my talents, and keep me interested and energized—as opposed to that job I just left. This is it; this is the one!*

So what happens?

Routine happens. Life happens. We discover our expectations were totally exaggerated. Just as many lazy, petty, uninspired people work here as they did at the last place. We settle into the humdrum. We start getting bored and frustrated. *Again*. Pretty soon we're checking our watch every hour, counting down the minutes until the workday is over. We're stuck in the mundane. *Again*.

The mundane job is why so many of us wake up on Monday morning with a sense of dread. We drag ourselves out of bed, then hit the train or the highway for the commute with resignation, like we're headed for bypass surgery. Here in LA, we are perpetually miserable as we endure the assault of the unending traffic jam. The whole idea of Monday through Friday becomes a source of anguish and disappointment.

Too many of us are imprisoned by a shortsightedness that keeps us on the treadmill. I have a friend, an award-winning journalist, who told me an instructive story from the beginning of his career. While still in college at a prestigious Ivy League school, he was giddy when he got a summer internship at the newspaper he used to deliver as a boy in his medium-size hometown. He showed up on the first day enthusiastic and eager to show his new editors what he could do. At an orientation he met the other intern who would be working alongside him. She attended a different Ivy League school, and he noticed right away that she was not happy to be there. He learned that several of her friends had landed internships at the *Wall Street Journal*, while that paper had turned her down. She was bitter about the *Journal*'s rejection and disappointed she would be spending the summer at a much smaller paper that she considered beneath her.

Throughout the course of the summer, this girl exuded an air of disgust with the place, giving every editor the impression that she felt like she was slumming, trapped in a dungeon she didn't deserve. The editors, offended by her obnoxious arrogance, all made fun of her behind her back. At the same time, my friend worked extra hard to make a great impression, in the process getting several plum assignments and even a couple of front-page bylines. Though he was tempted at times to tell his colleague she was messing up, my friend kept his comments to himself. He also became fairly close to the editor-in-chief, who was the young heir to his family's newspaper fortune, which was considerable since they owned a chain of papers across the United States.

When the summer was over, my friend and the woman went their separate ways. Upon graduation the following year, my friend got another internship at a well-respected newspaper in a part of the country he had never been. He did great work there, and when the six-month internship was over, the paper decided they wanted him to stay on staff. But they didn't change his salary, continuing to pay him as an intern while he did the work of a regular staff reporter. My friend grew frustrated eating tuna fish for dinner every night because it was the only thing he could afford. He also didn't like the city very much and longed to return home. One day on a whim he called the young editor-in-chief at his hometown newspaper. After a little small talk, my friend dropped the hint that he really wished he had a job that paid more money.

Within a few hours, this editor had made several phone calls that resulted in my friend being flown back home and getting a job at one of the top newspapers in his home state. The paper was actually based in the town next to where his parents lived. It was a huge win-win for him. And he carried that lesson with him for the next three decades, remembering how much benefit he got from applying himself in this internship—and how the woman who shared the internship that summer, though clearly a talented journalist herself, had squandered any future benefit because of her offensive attitude.

It's a powerful lesson that demonstrates the value of having the right mindset in the midst of a situation that could easily be seen as mundane. When it comes to our jobs, our careers, our workplaces, we never know what our future path is going to look like. We must dedicate ourselves to making sure we don't get derailed by letting the mundane turn into dangerous frustration.

Mundane to Magical

One of the most important ways to ensure you don't get trapped in the mundane is to have the *correct expectations* for your job, and one way you can do that is by not expecting that you will be in the job for the rest of your life. Some things are for a reason or a season. If you're behind the counter at Taco Bell or selling jeans at The Gap, working at an Amazon warehouse or at a Texaco gas station, the job doesn't have to meet your magical hopes that it will lead to exceptional prosperity. The job you have now can be just the first rung on your ladder to success. As an illustration, I turn to the well-documented employee training conducted by two fast-food chains, Chick-fil-A and In-N-Out Burger.[1] Walk into either chain and you'll quickly notice that their employees appear to be far happier and more enthusiastic about their jobs than at competitive chains like McDonald's and Burger King. Developing a positive mindset among their employees is a big part of their philosophies, and they promote the idea that the job is building character, a stepping-stone on the way to what's next. The companies know most of their employees are not going to spend their entire lives working in the restaurants, but they still try to make them happy—by paying them more, helping them with personal problems, creating tuition assistance programs to help them further their educations. As a result, both of these restaurants are at the top of the list of most profitable fast-food franchises, far ahead of many of their competitors.

It's interesting to note that most of these restaurants are staffed by young folks, because I know millennials and Gen Z have gained a reputation in many quarters as bringing the wrong attitude to their places of work. I've heard employees complain that young people come in with outsized expectations of how quickly they might move up the ladder and gain more responsibilities but with a poor work ethic and a lack of investment and drive. Some of this is understandable, as the corporate landscape has changed so drastically in the last few decades that people change jobs as frequently as they get a new pair of sneakers. Companies seem to have much less loyalty to their employees, and the employees return the favor.

My father started at Bethlehem Steel at age twenty and expected to be there for his entire life before he was killed in the motorcycle accident. Those days are over. But we still need to go into every job situation with realistic expectations, a realistic perspective, and realistic goals. Even if you're working at a gas station or a warehouse, you can begin to transform that job from the mundane to the magical by telling yourself the job is preparing you for what comes next.

In my coaching I often talk about achieving the Uncommon Life, which is a life filled with magic, a life imbued with the Miracle Mentality. Striving for the magical requires you to be filled with the notion of an uncommon dream, one that is different from the norm, outside of the mundane. To get that kind of life requires uncommon patience, uncommon focus, uncommon faith, uncommon passion, and uncommon preparation. The very job you might be cursing right now as too mundane, too much drudgery, might be exactly what you need to prepare yourself for what's coming down the road.

I love to research the kinds of jobs some of the most successful people in our society had early in their lives because it's an instructive lesson for the rest of us. The list of big stars who worked at fast-food joints is extensive: Madonna (Dunkin' Donuts), Melissa McCarthy (Starbucks), Jennifer Hudson (Burger King), Eva Longoria (Wendy's), Rachel McAdams (McDonald's), and Gwen Stefani (Dairy Queen). Amy Poehler, Julia Roberts, and Barack Obama scooped at ice cream parlors. Nicki Minaj was a waitress at Red Lobster, Kanye West did retail at The Gap, and Brad Pitt and Megan Fox danced around in front of restaurants wearing a costume.

Dwyane "The Rock" Johnson was a dishwasher at a restaurant as a teenager, which I found intriguing because I was a dishwasher when I was fifteen. I worked hard in that restaurant, which didn't escape the notice of the people around me. To my fellow employees, I think my work ethic was a source of annoyance. One of the cooks, who worked literally seven steps away from me making steaks, would tease me all the time.

"Timmy, man, you washing dishes like you own this place!" he said to me more than once.

That became his nickname for me, The Owner. He would point out how hard I worked to anybody who would listen.

"Oh man, look at Timmy! Doing those dishes like he's the owner!"

But that's what I had been taught. Work hard and much good will come your way. It's the powerful idea behind more than one verse in the Bible. Luke 16:12 says, "And if you have not been trustworthy with someone else's property, who will give you property of your own?" (NIV). And then there's Colossians 3:23, which says, "Whatever you do, work at it with all your heart, as working for the Lord, not for human masters" (NIV).

These words and the principles they espoused had been ingrained in me as a kid. My mother would tell me all the time that if I was going to do something, don't do a half-assed job. If you work hard for another man's dream, if you work as if you are working for the Lord, you can create magic in the midst of the mundane for yourself.

My efforts didn't go unnoticed by the restaurant's owner, Mr. Anderson. He had worked hard all his life, rising to a management position in the postal service. When he retired, he had used his retirement money to open a restaurant, which had always been his dream. One day he pulled me aside and thanked me.

"You know, Timmy, I retired from my job and took this chance," he said. "I appreciate your hard work. You work as though you understand the price I paid to try to make this restaurant successful."

I soon received my blessing. I got promoted from dishwasher to busboy, which got my hands out of the water. At least five different restaurant owners tried to recruit me when they saw how hard I worked. Each time I told them I couldn't leave because I really liked working for Mr. Anderson. One day Mr. Anderson pulled me aside again.

"Timmy, I heard the owner from Jimmy's offered you a job," he said. "It's a good restaurant. You know, they're moving in right next to the La Mirada Theatre, and they're going to bring in some big plays there."

He put his hand on my shoulder. "Listen, you've been with me for a year. That guy is a really nice guy. He wants to offer you a job, and I want you to go work for him. You can't be a waiter here because you have to be twenty-one to serve alcohol. I told him you're more than a busboy so he's going to make you an assistant waiter. Let me talk to him and broker the deal for you."

I did as Mr. Anderson said and took the job at the other restaurant. I was only sixteen and an assistant waiter at a fancy high-traffic restaurant. The money started flowing in for me. The waiters were all in their thirties and forties, mostly Italian and Mexican men, and they took a liking to me. Even though they were only supposed to give me 5 percent of their tips, most of them gave me a lot more because I would carry their big trays and do a lot of stuff most assistant waiters didn't know how to do. It was a great lesson for me in how the mundane can be made magical.

Years later when I watched the movie *Big*, I thought back to my days in the restaurant during the scene where Jon Lovitz's character gives Josh, played by Tom Hanks, a hard time for working so hard at his job for the toy company.

"Listen, what are you trying to do, get us all fired?" Lovitz says to Hanks after he watches him enthusiastically pounding away at the keyboard. "Slow down. Pace yourself. *Slowly, slowly*."[2]

When you're toiling away in these jobs, you have to believe you're being seasoned for a reason. If you're not getting the benefits, rewards, and accolades you think you deserve, take the long view, not the shortsighted view. Maybe this is a season of your life when you are doing all these things as unto the Lord, serving another person's vision and understanding that eventually you will reap what you sow. Believe that it will come back around to you. Build your spot and life will shine a spotlight on it.

We don't have to look any further than the life of Jesus to see the perfect example of this. Jesus labored as a carpenter until he was thirty years old, likely beginning around age thirteen. He was doing blue-collar work, all the while knowing he was a king. We should take strength from that. When you are in a mundane job, it's okay to know you're a king or queen. But remember, Jesus didn't work with his hands for one or two summers; he did it for about seventeen years. Think about the uncommon patience that took, the uncommon faith to know that something greater was in store for him. He had to have uncommon focus and passion, knowing that what he was going to be called on to do required uncommon preparation. Taking that outlook into our jobs will be transformative.

Messy

Have you had the experience of being on the job and finding you are surrounded by a den of gossip and negativity? Have you been around coworkers who pass around nastiness about each other and badmouth the company and the bosses? That's what messy looks like. It often comes from a place of insecurity and fear about the future, uncertainty about whether this dead-end job is the end of the line. *What if I don't have what it takes to be more than this? If I start working hard, will it mean I've accepted that this is my fate?*

I love the story of the famous Buddhist monk from Thailand, Ajahn Chah, and what he said when he held up a beautiful Chinese teacup: "To me this cup is already broken. Because I know its fate, I can enjoy it fully here and now. And when it's gone, it's gone."

What this story says to me is that when we come to an understanding about the truth of uncertainty and inevitability, we can relax and be free. To throw ourselves into our present job, whatever it is, because we know it's not permanent. But, man oh man, do we have such a hard time accepting uncertainty. I believe a Miracle Mentality is necessary for getting us to this place of acceptance, which is the goal of much of the work I do, especially in Hollywood, where I am called on all the time to help people grapple with their insecurities.

I believe that's why I came into the life of the late, great singer Natalie Cole. I can recall a memorable early encounter with Natalie at an event called "Night of Inspiration with Tim Storey." It was one of the many events I've done over the years in Southern California and hundreds of other places, trying to connect with people who are searching for the magical. On this particular occasion, the great songstress was in the audience. She felt so powerfully touched by what I said that she sought me out afterward. Natalie clearly needed help. She had had an extraordinary musical career, but she was still wracked with insecurity. I could feel it, could sense that she was troubled. The source of her angst? Trying to match or exceed the success of her father, one of the greatest singers of all time.

Nat King Cole had a transcendent career, nearly unimaginable at that time in the boiling cauldron of America. Though he performed in an era of vicious racism and hatred, his talent was irrepressible. The first black man to host his own television show—though the show was cancelled after just one season in 1957 because Cole was unable to secure a national sponsor, surely due to racism—Cole was a fixture on the popular music charts in the late 1940s and throughout the 1950s. He won a Grammy Award in 1959, the second year of the award's existence, and ultimately sold more than fifty million records and had more than a hundred and fifty singles reach the *Billboard* Pop, R&B, and Country charts.

We see the celebrities we worship as so beautiful, talented, and successful, it's hard to imagine they could be filled with insecurity and anxiety. That their lives could actually be messy or that their insecurities are overpowering. But over the years I've discovered that having your essence, your very soul, judged on a daily basis by the rest of the world—or even worse, by Hollywood and music industry executives—can be incredibly destructive. In Natalie's case, add on the enormous shadow cast by her brilliant father and you can understand the source of her problems. She experienced tremendous success herself at a very young age, which only multiplied the pressures she felt. When she was just twenty-five, she had two monster hits from *Inseparable*, her debut album—"This Will Be" and "Inseparable"—which garnered her Grammy Awards for Best R&B Vocal Performance by a Female and Best New Artist, the first black female to win that award.

She had long battled addiction when we came together. We talked a great deal about what it was like to revere her father but also be desperate to escape his shadow. In effect, by choosing the same career, she was expected to supersize a legend—clearly an impossible feat for anyone. But it's a story that is repeated over and over again with the children of successful people. Often children decide to pursue careers in a field that's as far removed from their parent as possible, even though they may have inherited a great deal of talent. Natalie said she felt enormous pressure everywhere she turned—from the studios, the public, her family.

Natalie saw me as gentle, reassuring, *safe*—a word she didn't attach to many people. She would often tease me about the way I dress.

"Do you get out of bed with your designer shoes on?" she said.

Natalie had seen me invite people up to be healed at church and was ready for me to bring my healing powers to her life. She was searching for a Miracle Mentality, yearning for transformation. She was overwhelmed and distracted by the largeness of her life, and I realized we needed to return to her roots. That was the only way to help her escape the mess.

Religion had been an important part of her life when she was younger, a source of magic for her. Natalie grew up Episcopalian; her first husband had been a Baptist minister. But the distractions of a life in the spotlight had taken her away from the church. She was no longer attuned to what God was trying to say to her. She couldn't hear his voice anymore. We began to delve into Scripture, reading Psalms and Proverbs, probing the intent of many different Bible verses, talking about what they meant to her and her life. In essence, I was using the words of Scripture to help her reset, to open herself up to the signals from God and to his miracles. She told me the exercise was a revelation to her. I believe it brought her a great deal of peace as we cleared away the distractions.

A saying often attributed to Eleanor Roosevelt states, "No one can make you feel inferior without your consent." We were bringing the truth of those words to life within Natalie. She got to a better place because she decided to open herself up to change, even though I knew it wasn't easy for her. Celebrities can be incredibly guarded; I believe one of the things I bring to the table with them is trust. They feel they can open up the lockbox on their souls and let me in. Natalie was ready for the two most important steps in getting out of a mess:

1. She accepted that she needed to change.
2. She let down her guard and let the change agent come through the door.

While these two steps may seem fairly obvious, time and again I have come across celebrities needing help who weren't willing to take these steps. I had several meetings scheduled with Britney Spears when she was in the midst of her tribulations, but both times she didn't show up. I had two meetings scheduled with Whitney Houston and she didn't show up either. Many people when they are in the midst of devastation can be aware that they need help, but they still aren't willing to open themselves up to it. They're hungry, but they are too afraid to allow themselves to eat. It doesn't matter if the meals have been prepared by Michael Mina, Wolfgang Puck, and Marcus Samuelsson—three of the most celebrated chefs in the world. If they aren't ready to eat, the chef will be wasting his time.

I go back to Psalm 23: "The LORD is my shepherd." We must be able to tune our souls to the voice of the Shepherd, the voice of the Divine. In order to do that, we have to be *willing*. I talk about this word all the time in my sermons. You have to consent—a word that has gotten a great deal of traction in our current social and political climate. But in my experience, some people just are not willing.

Mad

If you're human, you're going to make mistakes. Man's fallibility is a foundational element of almost every major world religion, and religion offers us an opportunity for redemption when we mess up. Some religions build entire celebrations around the idea, such as the Jewish holiday Yom Kippur, the Day of Atonement.

Yom Kippur was the day when the high priest, considered the holiest man in Israel, made atonement for his own sins, the sins of his house, and the sins of all of Israel. The spirit of Yom Kippur is then spread throughout the rest of the year, helping to create a culture of transparency and honesty, encouraging Jews to acknowledge their wrongs. Even the etymology of the name *Jews*, which comes from the Hebrew word *Yehudim*, means "confession," making it an essential element of the entire religion.[3]

In Buddhism, monks must regularly confess their wrongdoing to other monks. Most branches of Christianity have some aspect of atonement and confession as part of their ritual, though perhaps none lean as heavily on the confessional as Catholics, who obligatorily go to a priest seeking penance for sin.

Though our religions build the expectation of sin and wrongdoing into their foundations, our society still seems to have a great deal of trouble accepting and forgiving mistakes—in ourselves and in others. It is the profit-making fuel of the entire gossip industry—exposing and ridiculing wrongs committed by the rich and famous. What would TMZ be without sin?

Because of our complicated relationship with human fallibility, we are so quick to attach labels to those who might have messed up. In fact, we seem to derive pleasure from it. People don't even have to mess up to acquire a label—we just like to brand others. It makes it easy to put people into categories, which in turn makes it easy to dismiss them. I think one of the biggest challenges we face as humans is learning how to reject the destructive labels that others try to put on us. *Single mom. Angry black man. Illegal immigrant. Model minority. Chauvinist white man.*

When I was in first grade, my teacher wrote down in her class notes that I was "disruptive"—a tag that has sunk many a black boy's academic career before it even starts. The way schools work, you get slapped with that label and it keeps following you. Year after year, a new teacher would see me and immediately think *trouble-maker*. If the slightest thing in the class went awry, surely Timmy Storey had something to do with it.

Unfortunately, as happens so often with damaging labels, I started to embrace it. I looked for mischief, practical jokes, opportunities to play the class clown—yet another mentality that has damaged many black boys in school. The label had tossed me directly into a state of madness, making me a major player in my emerging self-destruction. I was headed for a jail cell—or worse. But right before I hit middle school, a teacher named Mr. Probert entered my life.

Mr. Probert had a gift for seeing the world differently than other teachers. He also could see me differently. He saw who I really was. Where others saw a class clown, Mr. Probert saw my intelligence. Where others said I was "disorderly" and a "problem," he described me as "promising" and "gifted." Up until that point I had never had anyone describe me like that. After a while, I began to believe Mr. Probert. For the first time in my life, I started to get good grades and I paid attention more—I even started reading outside of class. After all, gifted students were supposed to do that. For years I thought the only way to get attention was to be funny, but I learned I had more in me. I had more value than I had thought. Mr. Probert helped me bring about a miraculous transformation.

Many of us are slapped with these destructive labels when we're young. *The pretty one. The silly one. The smart one. The complicated one. The shy one.* And for too many, that label is *all* we think we are. It defines, it sticks, and it limits. That's how labels work. Those of us whose work life has gotten to a chaotic state because of mistakes, missteps, and inattention may be dealing with negative labels that have been attached to us, making it harder for us to get out of the mess and madness we've created.

When we're stuck in the madness, it can be difficult to realize that our lives are basically a series of unexpected interruptions. And the quality of the lives we lead is determined by how we deal with these interruptions. This is never truer than when we're looking at failures in our careers. Over the course of an adult's life, we inevitably will hit bumps in the road, times when it looks like our careers may very well be over because of something we might have done—or not done. I saw this scenario play out in a big way with one of my friends, Duane "Dog" Chapman, also known as Dog the Bounty Hunter, who made an ugly mistake and had the label *racist* attached to him.

For those who have never seen Dog's show, which aired on A&E from 2004 to 2012, it focused on the efforts of Dog and his team—mostly family members—to track down people who had broken their bail agreements. The show spent considerable time highlighting the compassion Dog showed to the fugitives as he urged them to get their acts together and the interaction of Dog's large family, including sons and a daughter who were learning the trade.

I started life coaching Dog before he got the A&E show, and I was excited about how far he had come and how much he had grown as a person during our work. I helped him get a manager, who was instrumental in Dog getting two book deals. I played a key role in his life—until one day the sky fell on him. More accurately, Dog pulled the sky down on top of himself. Dog got into an argument with his son and repeatedly used the N-word to describe his son's black girlfriend. Dog didn't know the son was recording the conversation. When his son put the recording on social media, Dog's life exploded into a firestorm of controversy and attack. In an instant, Dog was labeled a racist, he started getting hate mail, the world lined up against him, and A&E canceled his show.

Since I had grown to know Dog so well, I decided to insert myself into the storm. I talked to the executives at A&E and told them, "If Dog was a complete racist, why would he have a black pastor? I feel he is uneducated and ignorant to the fact that these types of statements are not right, they're hurtful, and they won't work in any context."

The executives said, "This makes sense. Why would he have a black pastor? Would you be willing to go on television with him and talk about this?"

"Wow," I responded. If my response could have been annotated with emojis, it would have been the one with the big eyeballs widened in shock. "Let me think about it."

I talked to some of my friends to get their reaction to the idea. Suzanne de Passe, the legendary African American producer who is credited with discovering Michael Jackson, told me, "Tim, I don't think it's a great idea." She basically said Dog was responsible for the hell he was in, so it wasn't my job to rescue him. As much as I respect Suzanne and see her as a big sister of sorts, I began warming to the idea of interceding the more I talked to Dog. Distraught, in tears, he kept apologizing to me. But I didn't hold back. I went off on him, pulling out every profanity in the Book of Profanities—you won't find that one in the New Testament.

I yelled at him that he had gone way too far.

"I know, I know," he said.

"That's really offensive to me, what you said. But as pissed off as I am, I do not believe you're a racist."

"I'm not a racist," he said between sobs. "I've always cared about everybody. When I was in prison I was down with everybody. I was more irritated at my son, so I threw something at him that I knew would hurt him."

I believed Dog's story. We had been through so much together I felt like I had a strong sense of his character. Life is sometimes messy as hell. What do we do in those moments, when we have exhibited behavior that is immensely disappointing, when we have stupidly destroyed a career that took years to build? In Dog's case, we proceeded to take the steps needed to get him and his career back on track. His comments forced him to take stock, to think about the essence of who he is. He said something I felt was not a true representation of who he was, so I chose to help him convey that to the rest of the world.

I accompanied Dog on two shows, *Hannity & Colmes* and *Larry King Live*. Larry's show, which got huge ratings for that episode, was especially memorable. Larry took Dog through the details of what he said and why he said it. Then I heard Larry say, "Now we will bring on the man who solved this problem and changed the outcome, the Reverend Tim Storey, next on *Larry King Live*."

When Larry asked Dog what I said to him after the video had been posted, Dog told him, "Well, the first words he said I didn't think reverends were allowed to say!"

Because of my intervention, A&E changed their mind and decided not to cancel Dog's show. But I got a great deal of flak from the black community for helping Dog so publicly. I knew it was going to come, but some of the things said about me and to me still hurt. I am always willing to stand up for what I know is right; that's my style. Whether it's for Kanye, Charlie Sheen, Robert Downey Jr., or Dog the Bounty Hunter—these are guys I have come to know and respect. In many cases they came to me because they had personalities or problems that often caused them to step into serious strife. My job was to stand behind them and help them get through to the other side. To assist them by showing them how to access a higher power. If that meant going on television and telling the world that I knew Dog to be a kind and compassionate man to people of all races and creeds, that's what was required of me.

I am obsessed with the idea of the comeback. It has long been an essential part of my teaching. I believe it is my calling to dig in with people who feel like they have failed and put them on the road to a comeback. It is basically the most dramatic example of the miracle, the ultimate transformation. That's what I'm all about, showing people that miracles can happen to them too. I've done quite well with my reputation as the "comeback coach." All around us, we see numerous successful comebacks—even in the Bible. For example, Hebrews chapter 11 is known as the "great comeback" chapter. When you read it, you can almost hear the *Rocky* theme song playing in background. In that chapter, we see that David, Noah, Abraham, and even Rahab the harlot allowed God to change their weaknesses into strength. The Bible says they became powerful through patience and persistence. It is probably this reputation that has allowed me to work with some of our society's best-known examples of personal and career failure.

Magical Work

When we feel like we are stuck in a failing career, sometimes what we need more than anything is a *change of vantage point*, an adjustment of perspective, a re-centering of priorities. Sometimes that can be as simple as committing yourself to volunteering time to help people much needier than yourself and realizing your career isn't going as badly as you thought. I think this is God's way of making us sit silently, by focusing our attention outside of ourselves.

You may need a good cornerman. You may need an Angelo Dundee, the most skilled cornerman of all time. In every one of Muhammad Ali's fights (except for two), he had Dundee there in his corner, whispering or yelling in his ear, helping him refocus or adjust his strategy to figure out how to vanquish formidable foes like Joe Frazier and George Foreman. Earlier in my career I actually branded myself "the cornerman," highlighting the role I played in the lives of my clients. When we are plagued by self-doubt and negativity about our lives, our careers, our choices, it is essential we find some way to change our perspective. That is the only way we will be able to hear the signals directing our next steps. A great cornerman—a friend, loved one, family member, therapist, mentor, someone who knows you well—also can help you achieve this.

Because we put so much stock in what we do and that becomes who we are, people have a hard time separating career failure from personal failure. And with the incessant push to have more, to be more from society, most of us feel like our careers are short of what they should be. If we're not the boss or we aren't making a certain amount of money or we haven't founded a tech company with a multibillion-dollar valuation, we haven't made it yet. We can't feel satisfied with what we have done.

Of course, social media makes it all so much worse. We create these facades to tell our friends that our careers are thriving, our days are fun, our loves are conflict-free, our children are wonderful and talented. In other words, our lives are perfect. We are in a constant state of trying to make everything appear ideal. We look at our lives and know the images we put on Facebook and Instagram are often a complete fraud, yet we are willing to believe the narrative being pushed by our college roommate about her life's perfection. Hip-hop fans are undoubtedly familiar with the shouted proclamations of DJ Khaled, letting us all know that he is permanently killing the game: "I'm the best!"

We have three screens that team up like digital gangsters to indoctrinate us: television, laptop, and smartphone. Over the course of our day, the average American adult in 2018 spent more than eleven hours staring at one of these screens, according to a Nielsen survey. (The time for African Americans was more than thirteen hours.) During those hours, researchers have determined we are hit by an estimated four to five thousand ads per day. In the 1970s the number was somewhere around five hundred per day.[4] In the last fifty years American insecurity has become a bottomless profit center. The number of industries cashing in has exploded—from beauty to counseling, from health clubs to dieting.

The inescapable reality of modern American life is that we will spend all of our days running after things we are being told we want and need—and that these are the only things that will bring us happiness. If we don't ever get them, we are doomed to a life of failure and embarrassment. This is especially true in our careers. We must have the degrees, the prestige, the big salary. The world is screaming at us on a daily basis that we must get all of this right. It sometimes feels virtually impossible to turn our backs on the assault. But one of the major takeaways of this book is that we must train ourselves to turn away, to reject the unrelenting messages, if we're going to find any peace and wellness in our lives.

When we enter the workforce, we have to do all we can to keep the onslaught from seeping into our mindset—whether it's the message from ads that we're not good enough or the negativity coming from coworkers trying to make us doubt ourselves and our work ethic. As we discussed in the friendship chapter, we have to be careful when we choose the coworkers with whom we are going to spend extra time. We should look for people with a similar mindset and similar motives. People who are not trapped in the mundane.

I put myself in the shoes of people out there in the workforce all the time, imagining how tough it can get for them on a daily basis, praying for them to have the mindset to get through their days smoothly. I think about two Amazon truck drivers, who are friends and work buddies, out in the world telling people what they do and constantly hearing, "Oh man, those hours must wear you out! Make sure you wear a back brace 'cause my uncle threw out his back."

They're working on behalf of the richest man in the world, Jeff Bezos, pushing themselves every day to put cash into Jeff's account, to add to the reported $202 billion he was worth at last count, an unfathomable number. Working to build this man's dream might be extra challenging, but they still bring their A game, not knowing where this job might lead. They still need to encourage each other and lift each other up when the job gets challenging. They need somebody they can lean on, to tell them, "Hey, I'm on the same journey as you. This might not be easy, but let's keep flowing."

Smokey Robinson told me there were endless mundane days at Motown—and even some that were messy and mad. They would record and record and record nonstop. Every once in a while they'd get a big hit, but most of the recordings never went anywhere. Guys would complain all the time, "Man, we're doing all this recording for no reason!" But at any particular moment, Smokey encouraged them, they would never know when they were one step away from "The Tears of a Clown," surely one of the greatest songs ever recorded.

It's instructive to think about the concept of the side B. It's something younger people might not understand in the digital age, but back when recordings were on 45s, the song that was intended to be a hit was on side A and the song on the other side was intended to be a throwaway. However, many eventual hits were actually on side B. If you google "famous side Bs," you'll see endless lists of big songs that were not supposed to be successful. Here's a quick taste:

"We Will Rock You" by Queen
"Hound Dog" by Elvis Presley
"You Can't Always Get What You Want" by The Rolling Stones
"L-O-V-E" by Nat King Cole
"Do Right Woman, Do Right Man" by Aretha Franklin
"I Saw Her Standing There" by The Beatles

In fact, Rick James told me "Super Freak" was a side-B song. He was making the point that you have to work your side B as though it might be a side A because you never know what's going to happen. It's easy to apply that to a job that appears on the outside to be menial but could actually be the necessary step to something magical. Older stars such as Tony Curtis and Charlton Heston told me something similar, that they didn't see the fame coming so they just kept plugging away.

There will be moments when it feels like life has gotten out of control and you have no idea how to stop the bad news from over-whelming you. When you're feeling like you're drowning, you have to reach out and hit the reset button. Take a step back from the madness and ask yourself, *What was my original plan here?*

I have a friend in the restaurant business who had two failed restaurants back-to-back, one right after the other. *Boom, boom.* He descended into a mindset that looked a lot like madness. He had lost all of his confidence and all the moxie he'd had in abundance when I first met him. He told me, "I don't know if I can pull this off again." When I started coaching him, I said, "We need to ask, 'What did I learn from what did not work? What choices did I make that may have added to this not working?'" Then I took him back to the idea of realistic expectations, asking where his expectations had gotten out of control.

When he took an inventory, he realized he had decorated beyond his means, he couldn't afford the real estate he had chosen, and what he told his investors he would bring in was unrealistic. When the customers weren't coming, his investors quickly got disturbed and began locking him down. His mindset went from magical to a mess, and the restaurant slid into madness. Investors started pulling out their money; there were even a couple of lawsuits.

He decided to give it another try with all of those lessons as a guide. This time he had realistic expectations, goals, and perspective. He took the test and turned it into a testimony. Now he has three thriving restaurants and is about to open four more, all because he didn't get ahead of himself this time.

CHAPTER 8

Money

I'm always amused when I look at the Instagram accounts of many big stars. They might start the morning working out in the gym, then they're eating lunch or dinner at some swanky restaurant, and by the end of the day maybe they're on a private jet with another big star, popping open champagne bottles, living it up, on their way to Coachella or someplace even more fabulous.

How can anybody possibly compete with that?

Yet that life gets stuck in our head. That's the standard, the baseline to which we all aspire. If we don't have their riches, if we don't go to their parties, we are failures.

Financial insecurity is a very scary place to be—suffocating, terrifying, paralyzing. We can't get out of our heads. We run scenarios in our minds over and over—homelessness, starvation, living in our cars, having to ask for money to feed our kids. But I think a lot of the problems are created by our conception of what we need in our lives to feel complete. A new car may look wonderful, but is it absolutely necessary if our old car is still running? How many bedrooms do we really need? That outfit might look fabulous on us, but we have clothes in our closet already that look fine. In other words, we have to step off the chase, move away from the want, and focus on the need.

Earlier in my life I was definitely in the throes of obsession with chasing the shiny object. I was doing extremely well with my life coaching and speeches; I upgraded to a big, fancy house in Beverly Hills, and then somehow got lost along the way. All the lessons I had learned from my mother growing up had flown out one of my big ornate windows.

She taught us to prioritize family, to never forget where we came from, to not succumb to the lure of peer pressure. I had gotten far away from all of these lessons. When she called me, it would take me several days to call her back—whereas I normally would return her call within hours. I was putting my work first, causing me to skip many family engagements, disappointing family members who were looking forward to seeing me. She told me I looked tired and that she felt like I was starting to live a lifestyle that somebody else had chosen for me. She had nailed it. I was succumbing to peer pressure, lured into chasing after the shiny objects being displayed by my new, very rich friends.

Of course, as a kid I was still susceptible to the desire for the right gear. When I was about nine, I saw a friend of mine wearing sneakers I had never seen before. They were high-tops and all white.

"Hey, man, what are those?" I asked him.

"These are Chuck Taylors," he said.

I became obsessed with getting my own pair of white Converse Chuck Taylors. I asked my mother if she could buy them for me.

They were less than $20 but cost probably three times more than the cheap sneakers I had.

"Timmy, we can't afford those shoes," she told me. "We talked about this, remember?"

Then I noticed these cool jeans everybody had started wearing. An older student leaned over the water fountain one day and I saw the tag: Levi's. I added Levi's to the list of must-have items. I just wanted to fit in; I wanted the feeling that came with being one of the cool kids.

But we didn't have the means to get that stuff, so I did without. However, I guess a seed was planted: one day maybe I could be one of the cool kids. While my mother struggled to teach us that we didn't need things to make us happy, she also pushed the idea of working hard. Everything you do, you must do at a high standard. It was back to the Scripture, Colossians 3:23—"Work at it with all your heart, as working for the Lord" (NIV). I took that particular lesson out in the world with me. But as my businesses began to soar at age twenty-seven and I was making a ton of cash writing books and speaking around the country, the seed that had been planted with the sneakers and jeans began to sprout.

I bought my first Mercedes at age twenty-seven. At age thirty I bought my second, a Mercedes convertible. I was associating with high rollers, and I developed an appetite for the things they had. They were driving in fancy cars and living in spectacular houses; I needed those things too. For the first time in my life I was around wealthy white people. I wanted to feel like I fit in, so I needed the right trappings. The last thing I wanted to do was slide into a Nissan in front of them. I worked more hours, gave more speeches, did more deals. I overworked and overloaded myself because I didn't want to lose my membership to the club that I felt had now taken me in.

It's a Mad, Mad World

While all of us find our finances in the mundane or messy state from time to time, I think psychologically we are all in a state of madness. We've all bought into the need for more, more, more; it's become a national obsession. Social media has given us access to how the other half is living. We can see the lives of the Kardashians and Jay-Z and Bey and Diddy on Instagram. It's right there in our faces.

When I was younger, I had to turn on the television to fictional shows like *Dallas* and *Dynasty* to see what fabulous wealth looked like. I didn't get a true indoctrination until I was older. One day I was on a plane with one of my white friends and he pulled out a thick magazine that said *Robb Report* on the cover.

"What's that?" I asked.

"You don't know about the *Robb Report*?"

"No."

"Oh man. Well, just look at it," he said, handing it over. I flipped through the magazine and saw that it was a guide to the best shoes, watches, vacations that money could buy. It was exposing me to a world I had never seen before. This was the Bible for the fabulously wealthy. I decided I needed to learn Scripture and verse from this newfound Bible.

The wealth obsession bleeds over into so many areas of our lives. It infects our parenting, our love relationships, our friendships, our careers—everything we've talked about in this book is threatened by the corrupted idea of money. I found out the hard way how people think about money can have a big impact on your relationships. I was dating a fairly well-known actress with whom I traveled to Las Vegas for one of her friend's events. During the day she said to me, "Show me what you're thinking of wearing tonight."

I pulled out the two jackets I had brought with me and put them on the bed.

"No," she said, shaking her head.

"Why?"

"Tim, it's 103 outside. You've got a wool sports coat. And it's Calvin Klein."

"I know, Calvin Klein is good," I said. I think she might have rolled her eyes in response. I didn't care if it was wool; it said Calvin Klein, so in my mind it was more than adequate.

I picked up the other one.

"What's this brand?" she asked.

"I don't know," I said, looking inside. "But it fits well."

"Okay, try it on," she said.

I pulled the jacket on.

"You got that tailored?"

"No, it's just off the rack," I said. "It looks good."

"No, it doesn't," she said, shaking her head. "It looks like a tent! You can't show up like this."

"I don't know. I think it fits me well," I said. But I was now seriously doubting my taste.

She shook her head again. The jacket was not going to work if I was going to be her date. We went in search of a more "appropriate" jacket for me to wear that night. We headed to the fancy indoor mall at Caesars Palace. I saw the names on the stores she was heading toward and frowned. Prada? I'd never heard of that. Dolce & Gabbana? Hadn't heard of that either. This was 1999 and I was in my late thirties, but somehow I hadn't come across those names yet.

"Dolce & Gabbana is a good brand for you," she said. I followed her into the store. She started looking through the jackets. She pulled out a jacket in my size and grabbed a shirt to go with it. I got a peek at the price tags: the jacket was $1,100 and the shirt was $280.

No, no, no, I thought, this is not going to be good.

"Babe, try these on," she said.

With fear and uncertainty flooding my brain, I tried on the shirt. Oh my God, it felt amazing. Like I was wearing a Bentley. I put the jacket on over it. *Boom!* It was perfect. She started sweet-talking the sales guy, flashing her stunning smile at him. He already recognized her from her TV show. He agreed to tailor the sleeves and the back for free. I paid $1,500 for the ensemble and stumbled out of the store with her, feeling like I had just been assaulted.

She looked down at my feet. "Those shoes are not working," she said.

"Seriously?" I said. I was starting to get sick to my stomach. "These are some good shoes. I got them at Nordstrom."

She looked at me. "They're not that good," she said. She saw something behind me and pointed.

"Let's go to Prada," she said with a smile.

I felt sweat running down my sides. *What have I got myself into?* In the Prada store she picked shoes that cost well over $500. When I handed my card to the salesclerk, I felt an ache in my chest. I was scared to death the transaction would be declined. I exhaled when it went through.

I said a prayer that she didn't have a problem with my pants.

This woman had grown accustomed to dating men of means who could pay over $2,000 for an outfit and not think twice about it. After that weekend I did a moonwalk away from that woman as fast as I could. I knew I had gotten in over my head. But I pledged I would never be in a position again to be fearful my card would be declined. So I stepped away from that relationship vowing to work even harder.

It took me quite a few more years before I began to see that magical is not a place or a price tag.

How Much Is Enough?

The word *enough* means "sufficient, adequate, ample," but getting to that mental sweet spot where we accept that we have enough can be challenging—especially when we're young and impressionable.

My attraction to shiny things led me to buy a $6 million house that was way above my means. I was with a friend who got the brilliant idea that he wanted to show me this house that was sitting empty. As we walked through the house, he was constantly bending my ear as he pointed out its many features.

"Oh my God, this is you, Tim!" he said. "Could you imagine the get-togethers you could have here?"

We went out to the back, and I saw the waterfall and the infinity pool. It was gorgeous.

"Picture the barbecues," my friend said.

He had called the Realtor, an acquaintance of his, to meet us there. The real estate agent was just as effusive as he was.

"Oh, this has Tim Storey written all over it," the agent said.

He leaned toward me conspiratorially. "A lot of people want this house, but I will hold it for you."

I got on the phone with my financial guy. Even though I was making good money, he said, "It's a biiiig stretch."

"But I got all this stuff coming in," I said, reeling off several deals I was expecting to sign.

Right after I bought the house, three of the four deals fell through. To keep up with the mortgage, I had to work constantly. I was running around the world speaking at conferences and selling books and CDs to pay for a house I only slept in maybe five days a month, if I was lucky.

As I got older, I began to see that my priorities had turned upside down. The things I thought I needed were not needs at all—and they had nothing to do with my level of happiness and satisfaction. I learned how much was enough for me: I'm able to pay my bills, save some money every month, go on a quality vacation, and have a car that's reliable and comfortable. That's it. I didn't need a house with seven bedrooms, an elevator, a waterfall, and an infinity pool.

Magic Money

Remarkably, the people I encountered over the years who seemed to be living the most magical lives didn't have a lot of money. The whole idea of money seemed almost irrelevant to them. I would walk away from them feeling somewhat envious, thinking, *Man, how do I get some of that?*

Because of my religious background, I've had numerous occasions to spend time with monks. Their lives are so simple, so peaceful, so filled with contentment. The Miracle Mentality oozes from their every pore. They are happy and peaceful simply being of service to others.

I had a similar experience with my mailman, who exuded a jolly air on a daily basis.

"Why are you always whistling?" I said about two years into his time serving my house.

He tilted his head to the side. "You know, I never really thought about it."

"To me whistling means you're kind of happy," I said.

"Oh no, I am happy," he responded, nodding.

"How long have you been a mailman?"

"Twenty years," he said.

"Do you like it?"

He smiled. "I love it."

"Tell me one thing you love about it."

He smiled again. "The fresh air. I'm outside. I'm helping people."

"How are you helping people?"

"Somebody always needs that check," he said, chuckling. "Somebody needs that mail. Somebody needs that letter from somebody."

This was a couple decades ago, when people actually wrote letters.

"It gives me a good feeling," he continued.

"Job satisfaction?"

"Yes, yes. I love it."

The monk and the mailman were living in their magic without chasing the madness. The first step on the path to that kind of magic is for you to determine how much is enough. You have to go in deep, not skirt the surface.

- What do I need for a monthly budget?
- Can my monthly budget be modified?
- Has excess secretly crept into my monthly budget?
- What are some luxuries I've let into my life that I really can't afford?

I work with a lot of clients who have gone through divorce. So many ex-husbands get riled up when they complain about the "maintenance" money they have to pay their exes to allow them to keep living the same standard of life. That word *standard* can drive people crazy. "Does it really mean I have to pay for her monthly massages and waxes?" I hear it all the time.

When I did that level of self-assessment in my own life, I fled that overpriced Beverly Hills mansion as soon as I could. I'll be honest—I did have some withdrawal pains, like I had stopped eating sugar. But eventually I got over it. People who didn't know I had moved would point to me while talking to someone else and say, "Oh, you should see Tim Storey's house! It's crazy!" Sometimes I would correct them, but other times I'd just shrug and let it go.

I was gaining a better sense of who I was. I was still driving a fancy car at the time, a Porsche 911 Carrera 4, but that started to feel off to me as well. This popular spiritual leader, teaching people to put aside the superficial and delve deeper for the magic, rolling up to these Beverly Hills hotspots in a black Porsche with custom-made lowered rims? I was experiencing some dissonance. I told myself, "I'm going to take it so far down it's going to shock people."

With perfect timing, I spent a few days with an extremely wealthy guy in Chicago who was living in the Waldorf-Astoria. As we stood out front, they pulled his car around. I was startled when I saw it was a white Mini Cooper, the largest one they made. It almost looked like a station wagon. This black man had done well in finance; I expected something flashier.

"Whoa!" I said when we got in the car. "This kind of shocks me."

"What do you mean?" he said.

"I saw you in a Bentley," I said.

He smiled. He was about sixty-seven, very elegant. "Oh, I used to have a Bentley."

"So how did you get to the Mini Cooper?"

He shrugged. "It's nimble. I can park it anywhere. I can turn easily." He turned toward me. "You need to get yourself one."

"A Mini Cooper?" I said, incredulous. "I wouldn't look good."

"Oh no, you'd look good," he said.

When I got back to LA, I thought a great deal about that conversation. Two weeks later I found myself pulling into a Mini Cooper dealership to look around. A couple hours later I drove out with the exact same white one my colleague drove. Cars were my thing—I had owned Porches and Mercedes-Benzes. But when I started to reassess, I realized more simplicity felt better to me. Okay, I now drive a BMW, so I didn't go the way of the monks. But I'm no longer trying to keep up with the Joneses. In LA, the Joneses will send you to the poorhouse.

CHAPTER 9

Health

Though science and spirituality have had a somewhat fraught relationship, I am consistently amazed and inspired by how much science actually supports the idea of a Miracle Mentality. I've seen the astounding extent to which scientists say our minds can change the functioning and even the form of our bodies. A mind that firmly believes in the power to heal can actually bring healing about—and there is a big pile of scientific research to back this up.[1]

A prime example of this is the placebo effect. For the last sixty years or so, scientists have noted that if they carried out experiments using two groups—one that actually received the medical treatment and another that was led to believe it received the treatment but had actually gotten an inert substance—many subjects who didn't receive the medicine would report it had an effect. Their pain had been alleviated or even disappeared, just as it had in the group that had been given the medicine. Scientists realized as long as people thought they had received an actual medical treatment, often their minds would bring about healing effects in their bodies. Researchers have duplicated the placebo effect in conditions ranging from acne to erectile dysfunction to ulcers to multiple sclerosis to arthritis. They even found that when they took images of the brains of patients who had received the inert substances, real and measurable physiological changes often occurred. For instance, if a patient got a placebo that was supposed to be a painkiller, the imaging revealed that chemicals had been released in their brain, resulting in decreased activity in the parts of the brain associated with pain.

I am continually thrilled by how much science has provided proof of the power of the Miracle Mentality. What science has shown is that when our minds are open to miracles, we can bring them about.

I speak every year at a major religious conference in Phoenix. It's advertised as a "Miracle Service with Tim Storey." Attendees are told it's an opportunity to have me pray for miracles to come into people's lives. As you can imagine, it's a very hot ticket. As many studies have demonstrated, a majority of Americans believe people can be physically healed by God—66 percent of American adults, according to a 2016 poll by the Barna Group, an influential firm that specializes in tracking faith in America. That figure includes 87 percent of evangelicals, 61 percent of practicing Christians, 55 percent of African Americans, 29 percent of whites, and 26 percent of Hispanics.[2]

The auditorium seats about 3,500 people, and when I spoke there two years ago the house was packed. I preached about God being a miracle worker, then I waded through the crowd and felt compelled to lay hands on a number of people I was sensing needed to be healed. It was a fantastic night. As I was walking out of the building, I felt a hand on my arm. I looked up and saw that it belonged to a middle-aged woman, probably Hispanic. She was frantic. The ushers gathered around, a bit concerned by her demeanor.

"What do you need, miss?" I asked her.

"My daughter is dying of leukemia," she told me, her voice trembling. "She's in the hospital. We tried to get her released for a few hours to come here, but they wouldn't let her leave."

She was staring in my face with a stricken look. "I thought maybe you could talk to her on FaceTime? To pray for her? I believe God will use you to heal her."

She said it with such certainty. Such faith. Talk about pressure! But when she was telling me this, I was feeling even more suffused than usual with faith after the meeting I had just had with 3,500 people.

"Get her on FaceTime," I said without hesitation.

When she handed me the phone a moment later, I found myself staring into the face of a young lady, probably about twenty-five, with a bald head and a look of expectation. Clearly this young lady had faith too. It may have been the last thing she was grasping on to.

"God is going to heal you and reverse this," I told her. "You are too young to die. You are not going to die right now. You are going to be healed."

By now the girl was sobbing. I handed the phone back to her mother, who was also sobbing. I walked out of the building, rushing to the airport so I could get back to LA for the Sunday service at my church. Two years later, this past August, I was back in Phoenix to do another "Miracle Service with Tim Storey." It went fabulously once again. As I was walking through the crowd afterward, a lady who was crying hysterically approached me.

"I've been trying to talk to you for two years!" she said. "You healed my daughter!"

"What?" I asked. "What happened?"

"She got healed of leukemia when you prayed for her! Two years ago!"

"Is she here?" I asked.

"Yes! She's right over there." The daughter rushed over and hugged me for a long time, sobbing uncontrollably. They proceeded to tell me that right after our FaceTime call, she went into remission. That family needed a miracle, a supernatural intervention from a higher power into the natural affairs of women and men. They had a Miracle Mentality, an all-consuming faith in the power of God.

Often people will tell me they like everything about me and my message, but they don't like all the faith healing stuff. I recognize that it makes some people uncomfortable; they are not ready to stretch their minds and their belief systems to allow for the possibility of supernatural interventions. Miracles. But what I tell them is I don't see myself as a faith healer. I'm just a man who believes God does miracles, and I try to help people tap into that power.

We're All Messy

When it comes to Americans and our health, there's a remarkable consistency in how much we complain about it and how little we actually do about it. Most of us know we need to lose a few pounds, but we have a difficult time pushing away from the table or turning away from the doughnuts or ice cream. According to the CDC, 42.4 percent of the US adult population met the definition of obese in 2018; 9.2 percent met the definition of severe obesity. (Obesity is defined as a BMI of 30 or more, while severe obesity is a BMI of 40 or more.)[3] Clearly we're not paying close enough attention to this problem, which can lead to serious health issues down the road.

Two statistics illustrate this uniquely American dissonance concerning our health. The United States came in first place in spending on health care in 2018, according to a Johns Hopkins study (followed by Luxembourg, Switzerland, and Norway).[4] But in the ranking of the healthiest countries in the world, the US was a disappointing thirty-fifth in 2019, according to the Bloomberg Global Health Index.[5] While that is a powerful reflection of the ineffectiveness of the US health care system, it also illustrates how Americans wait until the end of our lives to pay attention to our health, resulting in elevated costs. We practice too much procrastination and not enough prevention. We all need to do better, to move our health from messy to magical.

As we all know, we saw a catastrophic threat to our health during the COVID-19 pandemic. While we were suffering through the nightmare, I thought about how quickly and dramatically our health can go from messy to madness. About two months before the virus took off, I had booked Dog the Bounty Hunter to come to my church for an event. His veteran Beverly Hills agent cautioned me to buy a refundable ticket for Dog's flight from Colorado to Southern California because we didn't know what was going to happen with the coronavirus. When I told Dog about her warning, we both had a chuckle at her expense, noting it was her job to always imagine the worst-case scenario.

"Trust me, this thing's not going to go too far," I said.

Here I was, Mr. Life Coach, Mr. Visionary, and I was laughing about the virus and what I thought were his agent's unfounded fears. But the things in our lives that look like small messes can instantly ignite and turn into complete madness, which is exactly what happened with COVID-19. The virus wreaked havoc with each of the major pillars of society: family, government/politics, economy, education, arts/culture, and media. It was unlike anything we've ever seen, knocking them all over like bowling pins.

In my life coaching, I see a constant stream of people whose health problems seemingly ignite overnight and go from messy to mad. This guy not paying enough attention to that persistent cough—and one day discovers he has lung cancer. This woman going in for a routine breast exam—and next thing you know, she's had both breasts removed. Most of us aren't shaken into taking radical action regarding our health until it's a matter of our mortality. Our concern for aesthetics is rarely enough—we're not going to be able to maintain the stringent diet changes and discipline required if we're just trying to look cute. No, we have to fear for our very lives.

But it doesn't have to be that way. Some us manage to see our health with a Miracle Mentality, understanding that paying proper attention to our habits surrounding our health doesn't need to be precipitated by a looming catastrophe.

Magical Health

What does a magical state look like when it comes to our health?

I live in Southern California, so I am likely surrounded by a population that is a bit more diligent about the state of their health than the average American. In fact, my Southern California neighbors typically are the subject of national ridicule for a preoccupation with health that many people in other places may view as extreme. I must admit when I was younger, I also believed the Southern Californian obsession was about vanity more than anything else. I thought because of the prevalence of the entertainment industry, we were on a foolhardy pursuit for perfection. But my view has become much more nuanced over the years.

I've had many conversations with friends like Smokey Robinson and Berry Gordy over the years about their health. They would reel off an exhaustive list of vitamins and supplements they took every day that would have my eyes bulging. I couldn't believe it; I thought they were going overboard. But as I've closed in on the age of sixty myself, I have a decidedly different view of their regimen. As of this writing, Smokey is eighty and Berry is ninety—and they both look *fantastic*. All the measures they've been taking over the years have had magical results. I've come to understand they were being preventative and proactive—and that we all should use their example as guidance.

To start moving toward the magic with our health, we have to *value* who we are and we need to create a *vision* for long-term life. I am deeply moved by Psalm 92:12, which says, "The righteous will flourish like a palm tree" (NIV). Verse 14 continues, "They will still bear fruit in old age, they will stay fresh and green" (NIV). This verse inspired me to do more research on the palm tree, curious as to why that particular tree was chosen. I discovered palm tree roots, instead of burrowing down deep into the soil like other trees (such as the oak), grow in the top three feet or so of topsoil and spread out horizontally for extraordinarily long distances (as much as fifty feet in some cases), which serves to anchor and stabilize the palm. The nature of the roots gives palms an incredible elasticity, the ability to bend over drastically in heavy winds without breaking. This trait becomes extremely important when hurricanes blow into areas where palms predominate.

I saw this up close when I was stuck in Miami in the 1990s during a particularly brutal hurricane. The pastor who had brought me there had invited me to his big house to wait out the hurricane, but I opted to stay at my hotel on the water. I regretted that decision as I looked with widened eyes out the windows, which were shaking like they were on the verge of shattering. But what grabbed me was the remarkable sight of the palm trees, which were bending over so far in the perilous winds that they were practically parallel to the ground. However, they never broke. They had been designed to withstand hurricane-force winds. In regions like the Northeast, heavy winds routinely wipe out trees like oaks, whose deep roots can't keep them from being pulled out of the ground. In stating that people should be like palm trees, Psalm 92 is saying when storms hit us, we must bend but not break.

How do we keep ourselves from breaking? By practicing self-care, which means having the proper diet, exercise regimen, sleep schedule, and mindset. That's how we move into the Miracle Mentality, by taking care of ourselves in a diligent way—focusing on both the mind and the body. In order to live a magical, miraculous life, you must go beyond the norm—just as I saw with my friends Smokey and Berry. They have a real value for life, for their temples, and they have a vision for their own longevity. In the thirty years I've been around these guys, I've heard them talk about it constantly. And they do a lot more than just talk.

I think much of the rest of the country looks at folks in the entertainment industry and dismisses their lifestyle. I was in an airport a few years back, standing in front of the magazine rack next to a middle-aged white couple. Rob Lowe was posed on the cover of one of the magazines without a shirt and he looked amazing.

"Wow, look at Rob Lowe!" the woman said to her husband. "Look how great he looks!"

The husband snarled. "Well, what else does he have to do? I haven't heard anything from this guy in years."

His implication was that Lowe was some washed-up actor who spent all of his time in a gym and in front of a mirror. In fact, Lowe has been working steadily over the years. And I happen to know he lives next door to Oprah, so he must be doing alright for himself. But in the husband's mind, it was much easier to feel comfortable with his own middle-aged paunch if he could deride

Lowe's exceptional level of fitness. It's like the guys in the back of the room who make fun of the smart kid in the fifth grade who knows all the answers.

I can acknowledge there's a great deal of vanity at work in LA—how else to explain the ubiquitous ads for plastic surgery?—but there are many folks around me who have exactly the right mindset when it comes to their health. They know they have only one body and it's their job to treat it with as much care and respect as they can muster. I have come a long way in my own attitude toward my body. I wasn't always paying attention to this stuff like I should have been. But I went through the three-step process we all need to walk through in order to get closer to the magical.

First was the *revelation*. As I got older, I started talking to guys who opened my eyes to the need to take better care of myself. One of them turned me on to a wonderful dermatologist, Zein Obagi, who helped me with my skin. Others talked to me about improving my diet, drinking more water, eating less sugar. I'm not claiming I'm totally there, that I have fully stepped into the Miracle Mentality concerning my health, but I'm a long way from where I started. That's a key point—we all need to begin the journey to better health. Each step is crucial.

After *revelation* comes *conviction*; from conviction we get to *action*. The revelation told me, *Hey, you're getting close to sixty. You better start paying attention to your health.* For someone else, the revelation might come when they realize they are huffing after one flight of stairs or their favorite dress no longer fits. The conviction is a certainty that gets lodged deep in your soul about the importance of doing something, taking action. Once you're convicted, then you take the action steps needed to make a change. Once you are convicted, then you can say no to the pie, to the doughnut, to the sweets late at night. Conviction is a vital step, one most of us have difficulty making. Often we don't get to conviction unless we find ourselves in mortal fear.

I saw a friend of mine recently whom I hadn't seen in several years. I almost didn't recognize him. He's a white pastor I've known for years, but he had lost so much weight he looked like a different person.

"Man, you're looking good!" I said. "What did you do?"

"Yeah, it's called the heart-attack diet," he said with a bemused smile.

"What happened?"

"Man, I had a heart attack. I was so out of shape, eating awful food. But I realized I wanted to live. I got a nutritionist. I got a trainer. I changed my lifestyle."

He looked like he was glowing from within. He was the perfect example of moving from conviction to action steps, but something radical had to happen to get him there.

I have a great deal of respect for the steps taken by Rev. Al Sharpton to drop so much weight and get his health much closer to magical without being shaken by some health catastrophe. I can definitely identify with the church culture that led Sharpton and my minister friend to put on weight over the years—all those church dinners featuring endless plates of fatty foods and desserts, with seemingly never enough time for exercise. When you travel, a church mother is always trying to feed you. It feels rude to say no so you just keep eating. In his book *The Rejected Stone: Al Sharpton and the Path to American Leadership*, this is what Sharpton had to say about dropping 150 pounds:

> The basic fact underlying all my work is that every human life has value. But how can I preach the value of human life and at the same time preach that it doesn't matter what you do to your human life

with your diet? I knew I couldn't have it both ways. You can't say it's all right to kill yourself with diabetes and hypertension and high blood pressure and obesity but still parade around telling everyone to value all human life. If you value life, you have to value it in all ways. At least, that's what I came to believe about my own life. So that made me act to take control of my diet.[6]

Sharpton says the moment when he began to find conviction was when his daughter Ashley, five at the time, looked up at him with her innocent, curious eyes and asked, "Daddy, why are you so fat?"

"Suddenly, faced with a simple enough question from my child, all those black-church rationalizations sounded silly. In that moment, I began my long journey to become a living embodiment of the things I preached: the need for personal discipline and to hold human life in high regard, which, for me, started with prioritizing my personal health."[7]

The magical place for our health is being at peace, having a flow and rhythm to our body and mind. Traditional Chinese medicine has long understood the importance of this rhythm, with a concept known as *qi* or *chi*. Qi can be thought of in two parts: the physical portion that makes up the air, water, and food we take in; and the vital fluids and energy that flow through our bodies. When there is an imbalance or interruption in this flow, we experience physical, mental, or emotional ailments. Even people who aren't familiar with traditional Chinese medicine will complain sometimes that their body just feels *off*. They can't explain what they mean; they just know something is wrong.

I had a personal experience with this when I was having challenges with my gut, which in medical circles is often referred to as our second brain. I couldn't understand why I felt like I was in a fog—I couldn't remember things, my agility was off, and my mobility felt challenged. When I finally went to a doctor, I was diagnosed with "leaky gut." Also known as "increased intestinal permeability," leaky gut occurs when the tight junctions of the intestinal walls loosen, allowing harmful bacteria, toxins, and undigested food particles to pass into the bloodstream. Because my gut wasn't right, my mind wasn't acting right either. My rhythm was off.

When we have the Miracle Mentality, there is a smooth synchronicity between the mind and the body. Our rhythm is as sweet and effortless as if it were being ordered by Max Roach, the iconic jazz drummer.

From Addiction to Magic

I have spent a great deal of my adult life working in the realm of addiction counseling. It doesn't take long before you realize how vital a role spirituality plays in the healing process. The spiritual approach to treating alcoholism pioneered by legendary psychologist Carl Jung forms the basis for the 12-step program used by Alcoholics Anonymous. Jung essentially believed an alcoholic's craving for alcohol was the equivalent of a spiritual thirst for wholeness, for a union with God.

The next step in this thinking is that the only way for an addict to become well is to have contact with God—a need for spiritual contact that is a fundamental part of every human's character. For a myriad of reasons, addicts have lost that connection to the Divine and as a result have become miserable and sick. Their self-medication is a temporary relief; they won't be healed until they get that spiritual connection back. They have tried to replace God with alcohol, but that only leads to destruction and despair. In the

12-step program, a connection to God is so deeply ingrained into the thinking that the steps would be nonexistent without it; God or spirituality is explicitly mentioned in seven of the twelve steps. The program has been such a huge part of my life, not only because I have seen family members succumb to alcoholism but because of its connection to God, that I have even become the owner of multiple treatment facilities.

Sometime in 1999 I was told by a friend that someone wanted to meet me, but he didn't give me a name. I sat in a restaurant on Sunset Boulevard in Beverly Hills, waiting for this mystery guest. Around a corner came Robert Downey Jr., walking toward me with his unmistakable gait. Robert hadn't yet become the enormous superstar he is now, with franchises like *Iron Man* and *Sherlock Holmes* raking in billions at the box office, but he had been tapped as an incredibly talented rising star with his performances in movies like *Chaplin*—for which he was nominated for an Academy Award—*Soapdish*, and *The Gingerbread Man*. Hollywood had recognized his greatness. He also had a very public drug addiction that threatened to destroy his career and his life. He was a fixture in the tabloids, and his erratic behavior had gotten so bad that people didn't want to insure his movies. In other words, he was in the throes of devastation. Madness.

Some of the conversations we had are too private and personal for me to reveal publicly. But I can talk about the lessons I tried to impart to Robert. It was important for him to see that he actually was making progress. No, he wasn't yet where he wanted to be, but he wasn't what he used to be. We focused on the fact that he was growing and improving instead of obsessing over his flaws and the mistakes he had made. While he was disturbed that he wasn't perfect, I made a point of highlighting the areas where he was strong and growing stronger. That outlook turned out to be a revelation for him, the idea that none of us is perfect and to look instead at his progress.

For someone as talented as Robert, that quest for perfection was an extremely destructive force in his life. It's something that plagues a lot of talented people. But when you're waiting for perfection, it's a package that will never show up. You think you have the tracking number, you're sitting there waiting for the delivery guy, and . . . nothing. It never comes. I work with a lot of people in LA who are stuck on perfection—with the plastic surgeon's number on speed dial, trying to get Angelina's lips or Charlize's nose, and being horrified when they stare into the mirror and still look like themselves. No closer to Angelina. No threat to Charlize.

I know many people out there are lying prone with a house on top of them. As the nation deals with an opioid crisis that dominated the headlines, at least before COVID-19, I am reminded we have long been fighting the destructiveness of addiction in the United States, even when it wasn't grabbing national headlines. I know this because more than a decade ago, my brother died from complications connected to addiction. He had everything going for him—he was a handsome, charming guy with a great career as an engineer with McDonnell Douglas—but he couldn't get past his sickness. Watching my brother get stuck in the throes of this disease and then working with others in Hollywood fighting the disease has made me extremely empathetic to those who have this particular struggle. I find our society has become less empathetic rather than more, and it really pains me. I want to do everything I can to help people use rehab, prayer, an openness and belief in miracles, and whatever other tools we can offer them to emerge from their pain and get to their better self.

As I mentioned I am an active partner in several rehabilitation centers, and I have noticed a common trait among many of the people I encounter: the frequent use of the phrase "it's not my fault." They try to fix the blame, not fix the problem. They say they're in there because of a domineering mother, a dominant father, an overbearing boyfriend or girlfriend. The 12-step program takes direct aim at this thinking—challenging them to admit this disease is bigger than they are, to realize they need other people as support, to admit they need a higher power, to make amends and accept accountability. The AA 12-step program forces addicts to adopt a Miracle Mentality. It's the only way they can make it out, by having faith that they can transform.

When I'm working with people outside the centers who have battled addiction, I'm amazed by how often they keep returning to the behaviors and locations that led to their addiction in the first place. It reminds me of my frustration when I was younger and I got a scratch on one of my vinyl albums. Smokey Robinson's song "Cruisin'" drove me crazy because of the skip.

"Let the music take your mind . . . take your mind . . . take your mind."

I would listen to it over and over and idiotically be surprised when it continued to skip every single time. In the same place! The record had a defect, and the only way I could hear the rest of the song was to move the needle past the scratch. Sometimes you could fix the record by wiping it with a cloth, but those times were rare. Usually you'd have to get a new album and start all over again. (Interestingly, even if I hear that song today, decades later, I sub-consciously brace myself when it gets to that part and I'm surprised when it plays all the way through.)

When we are stuck on an addiction, we have to figure out a way to *get past the defect*. We can't turn in our lives for a new one, but we can change the way we do our lives. We can recognize what gets us in trouble and change direction before we get there. We can ask God to help us transform. We might even have to change the people around us. Significant self-reflection is going to be necessary so that we will be able to recognize our triggers and understand how we practice self-sabotage. But none of this will be possible without faith, without adopting a mentality that lets us believe transformation is possible in our lives.

It's Never Too Late to Reach for Magic

I first heard Rick James was in poor health when I was reading the newspaper in the summer of 2004 while on an airplane—where I seem to spend at least half of my life. Soon after, I got a call from a writer who knew of my work with other celebrities, asking if I would come and spend time with Rick. I told my friend Smokey Robinson about it.

"Man, that's really important," said Smokey, who had been a close friend of Rick's since their Motown days together in the 1960s. "Rick needs to see you."

Not only had Rick battled drug addiction for at least three decades, he had also spent time in jail for a variety of crimes. He had confessed in his autobiography to working as a pimp in his early life and had a long history of mistreating women.

I stepped into Rick's room at Cedars-Sinai Hospital in Los Angeles in the summer of 2004 and proceeded to have one of the most powerful experiences of my life. Rick had been raised in a religious household in Buffalo, and now, feeling death was imminent, he was desperate to make things right with God. He told me he had recently had experiences where he felt God was in the room with him, "but I didn't know what to do," he said. He had transformed to a Miracle Mentality and was eager for a supernatural connection.

I spent about forty minutes talking to him about his life, the things he had done, the mistakes he had made.

"Tim, I always knew better," Rick told me. "But I continued to do bad things. Now here I am dying, knowing I did these bad things."

"Rick, you have a good heart, but a lot of times you had the wrong people around you," I said. "You get around foolish people and you become a fool yourself." I had spent time while I was in school studying the Bible in the original Hebrew, and I came to an understanding about the true meaning of the word *fool*—somebody who knows better and continues to walk over the better they know. I told this to Rick and he agreed he had been a fool by associating with foolish people.

"How could I have done this to myself?" Rick said, sobbing. "I hurt so many people's lives!"

The tears were flowing freely now. "Tell God I'm sorry!" he said to me loudly, his pain evident. "Tell God that I knew better but I was a fool!" he cried out.

"Rick, God already knows because he's your father," I told him. "But I want *you* to tell him."

I placed my hand on his chest. He began to cry out to God.

"God, I'm sorry!" he shouted.

I could feel the presence of God. It was an incredibly tense, powerful moment. The two big guys in the room who were his quasi bodyguards began to cry. I began to cry. Rick cried.

Several weeks later, Rick was gone, dead of heart failure.

The lesson is that it's never too late to make things right. Hopefully it won't take most of us so long that we have to make a deathbed confession, but even that resulted in Rick having some peace in the end. It's never too late for a comeback. That's something more people need to hear. I often come across individuals who are grieving in their later years because of the bad things they had done. But even at the final hour, Rick made a miraculous connection with God, relieving himself of a great deal of agony. He was happy because he believed that although his life was possibly ending here on earth, the bliss of an eternal life was waiting for him in the beyond.

The lesson we get from Rick James is one we should keep with us, whatever life throws at us: it's never too late for the Miracle Mentality. Those of us who have made a mess of things in our lives, or whose bodies may be too broken down to be saved, can still find peace. We can still believe there are wonders awaiting us. It is never too late.

APPENDIX I

Chapter Summaries

Discovering the Miracle Mentality:
Chapter I Summary

- We are conditioned at a young age to believe in the power of miracles. In other words, most of us begin our lives imbued with a Miracle Mentality. But over the course of our years, things happen to us that cause it to slip away. Disappointment. Disaffection. Pain. Loss. Depression.
- The purpose of this book is to help you figure out how to get back in touch with the Miracle Mentality that buoyed you when you were a child, that made you an infectious carrier of joy.
- To have a belief in miracles, to be open to the idea that wonderful things can sweep into your life, all you need to do is look at your own life and the lives of people you know. If we start to probe, we can find evidence of the miraculous. I

161

believe each of us has been anointed. I'm a Christian so I use the word *God* to describe the Almighty, but all of the world's major religions speak of the healing power of the supernatural.

- The Miracle Mentality is innate. We were made in the image of God and—to quote Kendrick Lamar—we have royalty in our DNA. Through education, observation, and conversation, we all can draw out what's already inside us. Many of us unfortunately experience a lack of education, or a subpar education, and a scarcity of observation, and bad conversation, and subsequently our Miracle Mentality is suppressed. For many of us, that's called "life." But if you put someone in the proper environment, if you work to change their perspective on the world—adding the right kinds of education, observation, and conversation—you can change everything. They will "discover" the power of the Miracle Mentality. And it's never too late to bring about the change.

- Many times we are led to a Miracle Mentality because we are experiencing pain. The Miracle Mentality takes you into something I call the "uncommon life." That means a life lived outside of the ordinary, in an unusual manner. To have an uncommon life, you must have uncommon dreams, which requires uncommon patience. Many of us aren't able to summon these uncommon states until we are going through something that is extraordinarily difficult and trying.

- It's one thing to capture the Miracle Mentality when you're young; it's another thing entirely to hold on to it as you get older and are buffeted by life experiences. Most people get derailed on the way to becoming a grown-up. Therefore, the uncommon dream requires uncommon focus and uncommon faith. Two of the biggest things that happen to erode our faith are disappointment and disillusionment.

- Children come to us with a belief not only in the magical but in the power of love. They instinctively want to help other people, to show empathy and concern. But eventually their belief in love gets worn down.
- With the overwhelming problems most of us have to battle to stay afloat in this challenging world, sometimes we need something uncommon working on our behalf. The common tools won't get the job done. That's where the supernatural comes in, a belief in miracles. There are times when you need to call on supernatural, extraordinary powers to overcome addiction or career disaster or serious health problems.
- We all have the ability to draw on miracles to bring about the change we need in our lives.

Toiling in the Mundane, the Messy, and the Mad: Chapter 2 Summary

- Each of us lives in one of three states: Mundane, Messy, and Mad. But in reality, we all really want to live in the Magical. Magic moments aren't preplanned. Instead, they are like divine gifts, miracles that deeply change us, bless us, and transform us. The magical state is where we are living a life imbued with the Miracle Mentality.
- The Miracle Mentality is the state of mind, the principles, the strategy, the rules of living that set the conditions for magic to happen. It's a way to construct our lives for deeper meaning, bigger adventures, and more opportunities.
- The goal of this book is to help readers move from the first three states into the magical state so that they will create the conditions for miracles and transformation to enter their lives.

If you want something special to happen, you begin by setting the conditions for it so you are creating a space, an opportunity, a moment, where something meaningful can take place.

Mundane

- What is the mundane? The dictionary defines *mundane* as boring, dull, monotonous, uneventful, lacking interest or excitement. I define the mundane as the known things in your life, the comfortable, the regular. On its own, the mundane is neither positive nor negative. It's the neutral parts of life, the known quantities, the familiar, the comfortable, the everyday regular. But if you're not careful, it's easy to spend too much time in the mundane and not enough time challenging yourself, learning new things, and taking on new adventures. When we spend too much time in the mundane, we begin to sit, settle, and cement ourselves where we are.
- The mundane becomes negative when it becomes limiting. The mundane becomes limiting when it becomes the excuse not to grow, not to shoot for the magic, not to look for the miracle. When you only live in the comfortable, you begin to live life by default, not design. You don't take action, expand your capacity, and ultimately broaden your potential and opportunities—the places where the magic happens.
- To move forward and keep the mundane from trapping us, we need to take one of these three steps: *education*, *conversation*, and *observation*.

Mess

- What is the mess? The dictionary defines *mess* as the dirty or untidy state of things or of a place. I define the messy as the undone things of life. The things that are unkept, unmanaged, unmaintained. There is a concept in science called entropy, which says that all matter in the universe tends toward disorder. Translation: when things are left unchecked or unmaintained, they get messy fast. That's why our life requires constant care, good habits, and a desire to maintain order.

Madness

- What is the madness? Madness is the drama, the behavior that breeds negative results, uncontrollable emotions, or worse behaviors. The things we do over and over that doom us to repeat our cycles of failure. The madness can affect our relationships, our children, our health, and our dreams and aspirations. We have a difficult time holding it together and are often overcome by depression and extreme anxiety—states that can prompt us to reach for drugs or alcohol to escape.

Becoming Magical

- We have the power to push ourselves out of our mundane existence and to escape the messy and madness to get to a place where we are immersed in magical moments. When we do so, we have stepped into the Miracle Mentality. We are born with magical thinking; it is something we seek throughout our days in childhood. We play with Superman and Wonder Woman because we recognize in them a power to make miracles happen. Usually it is the adults around us who drain the Miracle Mentality out of our system.
- A scary but powerful aspect of living in the mundane, the messy, the madness, and the magical is that in those states we establish patterns and pathways we tend to follow. Those patterns are observed and absorbed by everyone around us,

including our children. That means we can pass these states down to our children. If we live most of our days in chaos, our children begin to see that as normal and they will live their lives the same way. But if we are often in a magical state, our children grow up seeing the beauty and wonder of magical thinking. They grow into adults who live with a Miracle Mentality.

- The new American Dream is to be famous. The intoxicating but destructive facade of fame seems to beckon every young person (and many not-so-young) in America. Fame has become a replacement, a surrogate, for magical. We can't escape our obsession with celebrity even if we hid in a cave. It's become a multibillion-dollar industry, feeding the American fascination with fame. A vast illusion is at the center of it all, propping up the entire enterprise: the idea that fame and wealth bring happiness, bring magic. The promise that if only we could be like them, we would be happy.

- But fame is far from a panacea. Celebrities get caught up in the same rat race as everyone else, chasing the next level of stardom or status or wealth. They, too, are desperately trying to find happiness, believing the next big movie or top-selling album will be the thing that makes their lives perfect. Magical. Even with them, the chase never seems to end. If even they aren't happy in their lives, what does that say about the chances for the rest of us, particularly those of us who use celebrities as our gauge of success or fulfillment? Just being good at your job will never be enough. Having enough to pay your bills won't be enough. We will always feel like we need more, more, more.

- Through the process of self-discovery, we realize we are all anointed in some way, gifted by a higher power with a calling.

We are able to access supernatural strength, to bring about transformation—to make miracles happen in our lives. But we can't stay closed off and turn our backs on it. We have to listen to the signals, slow down, and hear what God is telling us. We must have a Miracle Mentality if we are going to bring transformation into our own lives. It's sitting right there in our heads, just waiting for us to reach inside and access it. The time to start is now.

Trapped vs. Stalled

- When people talk about their lives, they often use one of two words to describe their condition: *trapped* or *stalled*. To be trapped is to be confined, to be held, to be kept. To be stalled is to be temporarily not moving. In that sense, stalled is better than trapped, because when you're stalled you feel like maybe you can get moving again if you get some gas or a push. When you're trapped, you literally can't see a way out of your predicament. The word *trapped* implies there is a ceiling above you, limiting your growth.

- Parents are a major factor in how high the ceiling rises for their children. Those of you who were lucky enough to have parents who raised you to soar to the heavens accessed a Miracle Mentality from a young age. Perhaps you were lucky enough to retain it as you got older.

Activating the Magical: Chapter 3 Summary

- Miracles don't usually happen miraculously. It's going to take some work to get there. Too many people imagine that fame and fortune will come their way due to the power of

Instagram, Twitter, or YouTube—if they can just get their likes and their followers to a certain point, they are certain they'll be discovered. That's not going to get it done.

How to Activate a Miracle Mentality

- The ideal state to bring about activation is a confluence of talent, opportunity, and desire. You need a healthy dollop of all three to step into the magical. You can have two of them, but missing that third will often keep you stuck in the mundane or messy. The word *talent* isn't about the obvious things, like Whitney Houston's fantastic singing ability or Jamie Foxx's incredible gift for impersonations and acting. It's about finding your passion—the miracle that's resting, waiting, inside of you. It's you recognizing the thing that God specifically created you to manifest. The thing you always knew you could do better than everybody else around you. Or the thing that always brought you great joy, but little by little you closed it off. Those talents and passions were a manifestation of God whispering in your ear, telling you this is the thing you were made to do. It's the miracle inside of you.

- What lurks inside many of us is the strong, debilitating presence of fear. *What if I try and I don't make it? I will have confirmed my worst fears about myself.* We all have to fight off fear at certain times in our lives. In the backs of our minds, we are grappling with the paralysis it can bring. Often, corrosive memories from our past get in the way, transporting us to the moment when it began to make sense to us to protect ourselves from disappointment.

- In Jeremiah 18:6, the Lord tells Jeremiah that he is the potter and we are the clay and he shapes us according to what seems best to him, just as the potter does. If you think of yourself as clay in the hands of the Lord, it's easy to imagine he has placed the magic inside of you. It's your job to let the magic out, to let it start transforming your life. The path to transformation is by *education*, *observation*, and *conversation*. One of these is present in most cases of transformation.

- If we know that each of us has been masterfully made, then we begin to understand that every day we wake up breathing is a magical day, filled with possibilities. And we think more deeply about our personal definition of magic and how it already shows up in our lives. You start with the small things that are within your reach but that can bring enormous value to your life. Once you begin to do that, you will be amazed by how much it opens the portal to larger, grander magical experiences. You don't need to become Beyoncé or Kim Kardashian to start accessing magic. Really, you just need a path to hope and joy.

Parenting: Chapter 4 Summary

- When broken down to the basics, the job of a parent is to guide, guard, and govern their child. If one of these isn't done adequately, the child is going to suffer in untold ways, likely well into their adulthood. As generations of therapists and developmental psychologists have noted, parents who fail at these three responsibilities often were not properly guided, guarded, and governed themselves when they were a child. This stuff tends to come back and repeat itself with a vengeance. *Guide* means direction, *guard* refers to protection, and *govern* is administration. We all likely know of adults who are suffering because their childhood was missing one—or in some unfortunate cases, more than one—of these qualities.

- If parents don't find a way to get out of the mess and the madness, they're going to pass it down to the next generation. There is a relevant phrase we use in the Bible world: "reverse the curse." If we have been burdened with trauma and madness from our parents, one of our most important jobs will be to make sure it ends with us. We must do everything within our power to bring up our children with the Miracle Mentality, to give them a chance at a happy, productive, healthy life.

- Psalm 78 is the Bible's lovely offering to parents, giving an exhaustive accounting of the miracles of God, the deeds he has performed, so that the next generation will know about the things of God and they in turn can tell their children. In the biblical construction, we're always looking three generations down; your actions will affect your children's children. We have to learn not only to believe in miracles ourselves but to teach our children to expect miracles. Once they learn how to receive miracles, then we teach them to release miracles out into the world.

Mundane Parenting

- What does it look like when a parent is stuck in the mundane? The mundane is the ordinary, the common, the status quo. It's the daily routine, the regular, the steady. Certainly, there's nothing wrong with having a steady routine, but the mundane has stages. It starts out as a routine, your regular schedule, but then it can lead to boredom, and boredom can lead to frustration. And that's where the problems start. When a parent begins to parent their children from a place of frustration, things start to go bad. Parents pass on that emotion to the children and a chill settles over the entire household. The children start staying away, spending as much time as they can outside the house—often in places where trouble is sitting right next to them, waiting to be taken for a spin.

Mundane to Magical

- How do we get from the mundane to the magical in parenting our kids? The first step is to understand that your parenting patience, your parenting energy, your parenting creativity, stem directly from how you are feeling about the state of your own life. We know instinctively that we don't give our kids the level of attention and care they deserve when we are feeling frustration and impatience with our lives. It's like the admonition we get from flight attendants at the start of a flight: "Please put the oxygen mask over your own face before you put it over your child's." In other words, you must take care of your own needs properly if you are going to be an effective parent.

- When you find yourself stuck in the mundane, you must take immediate action before it turns into boredom. You have to make room for the magic every week or you'll find yourself in trouble. What is the magic? It can be something small or something big—the important thing is that you give it some attention. You could schedule an exciting lunch date with a colleague or a friend at least once a week, where you go to a restaurant each time that you've never been to before. Even the process of doing the research to figure out where you will eat adds excitement and energy to your week. You might take a yoga class once or twice a week after work, or maybe on Saturday morning. Perhaps you can learn a new skill, or take up a new hobby. The possibilities are endless.

- You have to be intentional about scheduling things you know you will enjoy—just you, not you and your daughter, or you and your significant other. Something that's just for you. When you start to do that, your mundane lifestyle will be injected with a healthy dose of magic—and it will soon bleed into your parenting. Your children will be the immediate beneficiaries.

Messy

- Many families have been in the mess for so long, they don't even see the walls crumbling around them. When kids are raised in a messy environment, they get used to a certain amount of disorder. Things always seem to be in a state of flux. Nobody knows what they're eating for dinner. Nobody is responsible for cleaning up after themselves. They rarely eat dinner together at the table; they rarely talk to each other or ask about how the day went. There's a kind of selfishness at work in the family—everybody is doing their own thing, minding their own business, unconcerned about how their actions impact others. Keeping a clean house, a clean space, is part of a social contract, an unspoken agreement that family members adhere to. It's something parents are constantly reminding their children about, the responsibility they have to others. When that contract is ignored, everyone's mental health begins to suffer.

- When kids live in messy spaces—even though the kids may fight parental efforts to make them clean—they have a more difficult time focusing on tasks such as schoolwork, according to experts. Clutter makes everyone more irritable, anxious, and frustrated, which can lead to damaged relationships across the board. Living in the mess can also have more long-term effects on children. They are being sent a very strong message that messiness and clutter are okay. That kind of permissiveness in a household leads to a general lack of discipline that can easily follow the child into adulthood.

Messy to Magical

- The first and most important step in moving from messy to magical as a parent is to *wake up*. You have to realize you are raising your children amid a chaotic state that ultimately will have a major impact on their development. Once you have committed yourself to making changes, you must *take inventory*. That means you look at every aspect of your parenting and determine the areas you sense are less than ideal for optimal development of your child(ren).

- After you take an honest inventory of your spaces, you must *create an action plan*. This is perhaps the most important step. It's not enough to recognize the clutter and chaos without deciding how you will eliminate it. What is the theory of change that's going to bring about the transformation you need?

- In crafting your plan, the best way to accomplish your goals is with the assistance of *accountability partners*, who will keep you honest and disciplined.

- All the branches of the military have general orders that apply to anyone assigned sentry duty. Chief among the orders is this one: "I will guard everything within the limits of my post and quit my post only when properly relieved." The last part is especially essential: you don't stop guard duty until you are assured that someone else has relieved you. This should be taken to heart by every parent. When you have children, you must protect and watch over them at all times.

- Children are much more intuitive than we give them credit for, especially in reading their parents. This is how they develop their emotional intelligence, by reading their parents' moods. Children also become adept at picking up on people who have a magical aura around them, people who have the miracle mindset in abundance. When you live the magical lifestyle, you become like a walking billboard that people can read and sense.

Mad

- In madness, you lose your direction. There's a lack of peace in your life. There's a lack of rest. You have a difficult time getting to sleep at night because you are stewing inside a vat of bedlam. There's a paucity of hope; you've become so overwhelmed you want to give up.
- As a parent, you have basically lost control. You are no longer guiding, guarding, and governing your children because you likely aren't doing these things in your own life. The children are left to their own devices, essentially raising themselves—with often disastrous results.

Mad to Magical

- You can try looking inside to get out of the madness, but sometimes you aren't strong enough. Psalm 23 can be a huge help to you. It says the Lord, as your shepherd, guides you, guards you, and governs you. There are other ways you can bring shepherds into your life—living representations of the Lord whose presence gives you comfort and hope.
- If we are going to find a way out of madness, we have to turn our physical spaces into powerful places that can be an oasis for us and our children. There are also people who can have

that effect on us, who can bring us peace because they have that kind of impact on our souls. Whether we find them in church or in the house down the street, we have to figure out how to bring those sorts of people into our lives.

Love Relationships: Chapter 5 Summary

- Our love relationship is probably the most important relationship most of us will have in our lives. In effect, the health of our relationships—in parenting, with our partner, and in our friendships—is the most critical factor in assessing how we feel about our lives. When we are in the midst of a powerful love affair, the sun just seems to shine brighter. We are happier, and we have a much sunnier outlook each day. We develop faith that we will have victories in other areas. We start looking to win. When the love relationship is not going well, many negative effects, including poorer health, can occur. You start looking around, waiting to see what other disasters are going to befall you. You start seeing your life through the lens of the loss.

Mundane in Love

- Our love relationships are often the unwitting victims of the incessant sensory overload that is life in modern America. Sometimes it feels nearly impossible to keep the fires alive and another human being happy with themselves and with us when we are all being told we are not good enough. But despite the seeming impossibility of nurturing successful relationships, we still expect them to fulfill all our needs—and inevitably feel the inescapable drag of failure when they don't.

- It's extremely common in our love relationships for us to forget about doing all the things that brought us together and made us click in the beginning. Remember all the things you did when you first started dating your significant other, all the extra steps you took to make everything perfect? Everything was filled with magic. But then you stopped. The magic worked; he or she is yours. So you got comfortable. The planning went out the window. You aren't trying to connect with each other anymore. There's no overestimating how much effort it takes to keep a relationship from slipping from magical to mundane. It's not for the faint of heart. But so many things rest on our ability to keep the magic alive. A huge percentage of American marriages are likely sitting uncomfortably in the mundane, on the verge of becoming a problem, becoming messy or even mad.

Mundane to Magical

- From a biblical standpoint, your priorities in your family should be clear: God first, your spouse second, your kids third, your job fourth. Once that initial connection is made, it is incumbent on both parties to make sure the fire stays hot, to remain connected, to cultivate the relationship. That means plow the ground, plant the seed, water the seed, and reap the bounty of the harvest. *Connect* and *cultivate*. Cultivation in the context of a love relationship is all about quality time, quality conversations, quality intimacy. Because we typically started our relationships in a magical state, I think most people instinctively know what steps would need to be taken to get back there. Cultivation means to feed, to watch blossom, to protect, to care for. Every single one of these must be present in a love relationship trying to get back to magic.

- In addition to connect and cultivate, add a third C: *create*. You must go out of your way in love relationships to create opportunities for magical moments. The effort is extremely important. We need to regularly *take inventory* of how much effort we are putting into creating magic in our love relationships.

- In order to share any job, communication is crucial. When you sense that the magic has drained away, you have to talk about it. During those talks, you must be honest about what you think you're missing. Once you get to that point, you must *take action steps*. The list of fun activities you can undertake together is endless, ranging from tennis or bowling to gardening or jigsaw puzzles. The thing isn't as important as the time. Be creative.

Messy

- At some point, messy tries to invade every relationship. A messy relationship feels disheveled and disorderly—it starts to lose its rhythm. You got too comfortable in the comfortable. The messes begin to manifest in many ways—someone forgets their partner's birthday, an important anniversary is missed, one of the partners completely neglects an event that had been planned for months. In addition to forgetting, both sides start reneging on promises. Messy will soon descend into arguments, anger, and resentment if it's not addressed. Once you get there, the trip from messy to mad is dangerously short.

Mad

- Your relationship has descended into madness when you just can't ever seem to concentrate because your thoughts keep going back to home. You lose your sense of peace, which is one of the most important aspects of a successful relationship.

You're in the madness when you lose your sense of contentment. There is too much resentment and hostility to conduct regular relationship activities. You're too depleted, distracted, and devastated for the normal stuff to occur. Bad things start happening, such as infidelity and big-time disrespect. One or both of you become dramatic in the midst of the drama.

Messy and Mad to Magical

- In order to get out of madness, you're going to need help. It's a rare couple that can emerge from this on their own. Try these action steps:

1. **Reach out to God.**
2. **Find the correct counselor.** "Correct" means someone who is going to understand the nature of your crisis and know how to act on it.
3. **Partner with the right people.** If you're talking to the wrong people, you could be getting the wrong advice.

Friendships: Chapter 6 Summary

- If you want to have a clear idea of which life state you're in—mundane, messy, mad, or magical—all you need do is look around and ask yourself, *What state are my friends in?*
- We all have friends in our lives who serve different purposes—the party friend, the wise friend, the serious friend, the perpetually depressed friend. We often make subconscious decisions about what we need from a friend before we decide which one to call. A friendship is a pact, a devotion, a closeness, an agreement, an understanding. It's a relationship, a bond, a tie, an attachment.

- The people with whom we associate have a powerful ability to influence us. They have the capacity to affect our behavior, our character development, our life goals, our state of mind. Our family and friends are the most powerful influence on our lives. As such, you must ask yourself these questions:

  Are your associations lifting you up or dragging you down?

  Are the people you associate with the kind of people you would like to be?

  Do your associations have the Miracle Mentality?

- In order to have a magical life, you have to have magical partnerships.

- The Miracle Mentality can create uncommon adversaries. But in order for you to partner with power, you have to set aside any pettiness or jealousies. You have to find the common threads you share with someone who might have been an enemy or a competitor and understand how much more you can accomplish as a team, as opposed to foes.

Magical Friendships

- Magical friendships are the ones that can transform your life. When you have those kinds of friends, they download the Miracle Mentality into your brain. If you have access to people in your life who already have the Miracle Mentality, do all that you can to cultivate those friendships.

- We know many of our friends aren't prepared to move from the mundane to the magical, but we should still try to be a source of motivation for them. Pull as many as you can along the way as you begin to transform your life. Just don't expect everyone to follow along. You may need to let go of those who resist you—or at least temper your expectations. Call them up on occasion, have a great time with them, but protect your dreams from those forces who will try to destroy out of insecurity or envy.

Work/Career: Chapter 7 Summary

- The mundane job is why so many of us wake up on Monday morning with a sense of dread.
- When it comes to our jobs, our careers, and our workplaces, we never know what our future path is going to look like. We must dedicate ourselves to making sure we don't become derailed by letting the mundane turn into dangerous frustration.

Mundane to Magical

- One of the most important ways to ensure that you don't get trapped in the mundane is to have the *correct expectations* for your job. That means you don't start any job with the expectation that you will be in the job for the rest of your life. Some things are for a reason or a season.
- We need to go into every job situation with realistic expectations, a realistic perspective, and realistic goals. Even if you're working at a gas station or a warehouse, you can begin to transform that job from the mundane to the magical by telling yourself the job is preparing you for what comes next.
- The Uncommon Life is a life filled with magic, a life imbued with the Miracle Mentality. To strive for the magical is to be filled with the notion of an uncommon dream, a dream that is different from the norm, that is outside of the mundane. To get that kind of life requires uncommon patience, uncommon focus, uncommon faith, uncommon passion, and uncommon

preparation. The very job you might be cursing right now as too mundane and too much drudgery might be exactly what you need to prepare yourself for what's coming down the road.

- If you work hard at another man's dream and if you work as if you are working for the Lord, you can create magic in the midst of the mundane.

- If you're not getting the benefits, rewards, and accolades you think you deserve at your job, take the long view, not the short-sighted view. Maybe this is a season of your life when you're doing all these things as unto the Lord and serving another person's vision, understanding that eventually you will reap what you sow. Believe that it will come back around to you.

- Jesus was doing blue-collar work, all the while knowing he was a king. We should take strength from that. When you are in a mundane job, it's okay to know you're a king or queen.

Messy

- Messy often comes from a place of insecurity and fear about the future and uncertainty about whether this dead-end job is the end of the line for us.

- When we can come to an understanding about the truth of uncertainty and inevitability, it allows us to relax and be free. To throw ourselves into our present job, whatever it is, because we know it's not permanent.

- The two most important steps in getting out of a mess:
  —Accepting that you need change.
  —Letting down your guard and letting the change agent come through the door.

- Many people when they are in the midst of devastation can be aware that they need help, but they still aren't willing to open themselves up to it. They're hungry, but they're too afraid to allow themselves to eat. We must be able to tune our souls to the voice of the shepherd, the voice of the Divine. In order to do that, we have to be *willing*.

Mad

- If you're human, you're going to make mistakes. Man's fallibility is a foundational element of almost every major world religion. Though our religions build the expectation of sin and mistakes into their foundations, our society still seems to have a great deal of trouble accepting and forgiving mistakes—in ourselves and in others.
- You don't even have to mess up to acquire a label—we just like to brand people. It makes it easy to put people into categories, which in turn makes it easy to dismiss them. One of the biggest challenges we face as humans is learning how to reject the destructive labels that others try to put on us.
- When we're stuck in the madness, it can be hard for us to realize that our lives are basically a series of unexpected interruptions. And the quality of the lives we lead is determined by how we deal with the interruptions. Over the course of an adult's life, we inevitably will hit bumps in the road, times when it looks like our careers may very well be over because of something we might have done—or not done.

Magical Work

- When we feel like we are stuck in a failing career, sometimes what we need more than anything is a *change of vantage point*, an adjustment of perspective, a re-centering of priorities. Sometimes it can be as simple as committing yourself to others in the form of volunteering time to people much needier than yourself to realize your career isn't doing as badly as you thought. I think this is God's way of making us sit silently and focusing our attention outside of ourselves.

- *You need a good cornerman.* When we are plagued by self-doubt and negativity about our lives, our careers, and our choices, it's essential we find some way to change our perspective. That's the only way we will be able to hear the signals directing our next steps. A great cornerman—a friend, loved one, family member, therapist, mentor, someone who knows you well—also can help us achieve this trick.

- Because we put so much stock in what we do and that becomes who we are, people have a hard time separating career failure from personal failure. And with the incessant push from society, most of us feel like our careers are short of what they should be.

- In our careers, we feel like we must have the degrees, the prestige, the big salary. The world is screaming at us on a daily basis that we must get all of this right. It sometimes feels impossible to turn our backs on the assault. One of the major takeaways of this book is that we must train ourselves to turn away, to reject the onslaught, if we're going to find any peace and wellness in our lives.

- We have to be careful when we choose coworkers with whom we are going to spend considerable time. We should look for people with a similar mindset and similar motives, people who are not trapped in the mundane.

- You have to work your side B as though it might be a side A because you never know if that "throwaway" job could be the necessary step to something magical.

- When you're feeling like you're drowning in it, you have to reach out and hit the reset button. Take a step back from the madness and ask yourself, *What was my original plan here?*

Money: Chapter 8 Summary

- Financial insecurity is a very scary place to be—suffocating, terrifying, paralyzing. But a lot of the problems are created by our conception of what we need in our lives to feel complete. We have to step off the chase, move away from the want, and focus on the need.

- So many of us spend our days grappling with insecurity, it's one of the defining characteristics of our age. At a time when the world is moving at a head-spinning pace, when we have access to more information than we have ever had, we're always wondering, *Am I doing it right?*

It's a Mad, Mad World

- While all of us see our finances in the mundane or messy state from time to time, psychologically we are all in a state of madness. We've all bought into the need for more, more, more; it's become a national obsession. The wealth obsession bleeds over into so many areas of our lives. It infects our parenting, our love relationships, our friendships, our careers—everything we talk about in this book is threatened by the corrupted idea of money.

How Much Is Enough?

- The word *enough* means sufficient, adequate, ample, but getting to that mental sweet spot where you accept that you have enough can be challenging—especially when we're young and impressionable.

Magic Money

- The people who seem to be living the most magical lives don't have a lot of money. The whole idea of money seems almost irrelevant to them. Upon meeting them, we walk away thinking, *Man, how do I get some of that?* For instance, the lives of monks are so simple, so peaceful, so filled with contentment. The Miracle Mindset oozes from their every pore. They are happy and peaceful simply being of service to others.

- The first step on the path to that kind of magic is for you to determine how much is enough. You have to go in deep, not skirt the surface.

—What do I need for a monthly budget?

—Can my monthly budget be modified?

—Has excess secretly crept into my monthly budget?

—What are some luxuries I've let into my life that I really can't afford?

Health: Chapter 9 Summary

- To an astounding degree, science supports the idea of a Miracle Mentality. Study after study proves that our minds can change the functioning and even the form of our bodies. A mind that firmly believes in the power to heal can actually bring healing about.

- Exhibit A: the placebo effect. For the last sixty years or so, scientists have noted that if they carried out experiments using two groups—one that actually received the medical treatment and another that was led to believe it received the treatment but had actually been given an inert substance—many in the group of subjects that did not receive the medicine would report that it had had an effect. Scientists realized that as long as these people thought they had received an actual medical treatment, their minds would possibly bring about healing effects in their bodies. Scientists even found that when they took images of the brains of patients who had received the inert substances, real and measurable physiological changes were occurring.

- A majority of Americans believe that people can be physically healed by God—66 percent of American adults, according to a 2016 poll by the Barna Group, an influential firm that specializes in tracking faith in America.

We're All Messy

- When it comes to Americans and our health, there's a remarkable consistency in how much we complain about it and how little we actually do about it. We practice too much procrastination and not enough prevention.
- Most of us aren't shaken into taking radical action regarding our health until it's a matter of our mortality. Our concern for aesthetics is rarely enough—we're not going to be able to maintain the stringent diet changes and discipline required if we're just trying to look cute. No, we have to fear for our very lives. But it doesn't have to be that way.

Magical Health

- To start moving toward the magic with our health, we have to *value* who we are and we need to create a *vision* for long-term life.
- In stating that people should be like palm trees, Psalm 92 tells us that when storms hit us, we must bend but not break. How do we keep ourselves from breaking? By practicing self-care, which means having the proper diet, exercise regimen, sleep schedule, and mindset. That's how we move into the Miracle Mentality, by taking care of ourselves in a diligent way and

focusing on both the mind and the body. It's an acknowledgment that in order to live a magical, miraculous life, you must go beyond the norm.

- There is a three-step process we all need to walk through in order to get closer to the magical. First is the *revelation*; next comes *conviction*; then we get to *action*. The revelation might come when you realize you are huffing after one flight of stairs or your favorite dress no longer fits. The conviction is a certainty that gets lodged deep in your soul about the importance of doing something, taking action. Once you are convicted, then you take the action steps to make change—you can say no to the pie, to the doughnut, to the sweets late at night. Conviction is a vital step that most of us have difficulty making. Often, we don't get to conviction unless we find ourselves in mortal fear.

- When we have the Miracle Mentality, there is a smooth synchronicity between the mind and body. Our rhythm is sweet and effortless.

From Addiction to Magic

- The spiritual approach to treating alcoholism pioneered by legendary psychologist Carl Jung forms the basis for the 12-step program used by Alcoholics Anonymous. Jung essentially believed an alcoholic's craving for alcohol is the equivalent of a spiritual thirst for wholeness, for a union with God. The next step in this thinking is that the only way for an addict to become well is to have a relationship with God—a need for spiritual contact that is a fundamental part of every human's character. For a myriad of reasons, addicts have lost that connection to the Divine and as a result have become miserable and sick.

- The quest for perfection can be an extremely destructive force, one that plagues a lot of talented people. But when you're waiting for perfection, it's a package that will never show up.
- When we are stuck in an addiction, we have to figure out a way to *get past the defect.* We can't turn in our lives for a new one, but we can change the way we do our lives. We can recognize the steps that get us in trouble and change direction before we get there. We can ask God to help us transform. We might even have to change the people around us. Significant self-reflection is going to be necessary so that we will be able to recognize our triggers, to understand how we practice self-sabotage. But none of this will be possible without faith, without adopting a mentality that lets you believe that transformation is possible in your life.

It's Never Too Late to Reach for Magic

- For those of us who have made a mess of things in our lives or whose bodies may be too broken down to be saved, we can still find peace. We can still believe that there are wonders awaiting us. It is never too late.

APPENDIX 2

The Miracle Mentality Total Mindset Assessment

Want to unlock the magic in your life?

Take the Miracle Mentality Total Mindset Assessment.

Here's how the Total Mindset Assessment works: You'll be asked a series of questions designed to assess the current state of your Miracle Mindset. Each question will ask you to choose a state from Madness to Magic that most accurately describes you. You'll then be given three options to clarify how much that state best describes how you are doing.

When you're finished, you'll be given a personal Miracle Mindset score on a scale from 0 to 110. This score will show you what state you're currently in and how you can move your life from the madness, messy, and mundane to the magic!

Total Assessment Time: 5 to 10 minutes

TOTAL MINDSET ASSESSMENT

Question Overview

1. How would you describe the state of your life? (Score 0–11)
2. How much "magic" do you experience regularly? (Score 0–11)
3. How do you feel about your future? (Score 0–11)
4. How close are you to reaching your dreams? (Score 0–11)
5. How much quality time do you spend with your family/kids? (Score 0–11)
6. How content are you with your love life? (Score 0–11)
7. Do you have friends who are there for you? (Score 0–11)
8. What is the trajectory of your career? (Score 0–11)
9. What is your personal financial situation? (Score 0–11)
10. How would you describe your self-care? (Score 0–11)

Total Score Range = 0–110

Score Categories

- 0–28: Madness
- 29–56: Messy
- 57–84: Mundane
- 85–110: Magical

Your Personal Mentality Type

Level One: The Madness (0–28)
THE DRAMATIC ALL-STAR

In just about every area, things are a little crazy. Right now there is very little security, people, or finances to count on. The direction of your life seems unclear and somewhat foggy. You feel stuck in your setbacks and are struggling to move forward freely. Despite the struggle, you have a strong desire to change, grow, and learn. The fact that you invested in yourself by reading this book shows that you are tired of the drama and ready to reach for the magic.

Level Two: The Messy (29–56)
THE HOT MESS

Even though some things are looking up, overall, life is still messy. You might have a job—but it's not the best job, and it's not much fun either. You might have family and friends—but you don't get along with them very well and don't have much fun together. You might have plans for the future—but you're nowhere close to where you want to be financially or in your career. You have *some* direction, but you spend so much time in the mess that you feel it's keeping you from the magic and from making real progress physically, spiritually, mentally, financially, and relationally. You need some help.

Level Three: The Mundane (57–84)
"I'LL HAVE THE REGULAR"

Right now things are comfortable. So far you've been able to handle most of what life has thrown at you. Things are fairly organized and nothing in your life is falling apart. You have steady relationships with little to no drama. You've developed good habits that bring order to your life. But . . . you feel *stuck*. Things are fine, but your life is not very exciting. Everything has gotten comfortable and predictable. That predictability has led to feelings of being bored and uninspired. You are living life in neutral with little drive pushing you forward.

Level Four: The Magical (85–110)
THE MIRACLE WORKER

It's official: you've cracked the code on life. You have not only mastered personal self-discipline and healthy relationships, you are now living in the bonus round! However, even though you experience miracles everywhere you go, you know you are still a work in progress. There is still room to grow, places to go, and people to meet. You have experienced a taste of uncommon results and now want to commit yourself to an uncommon life.

Assessment

1. How would you describe the state of your life?

Madness

In just about every area, things are a little crazy. Right now there is very little security, people, or finances to count on. The direction of your life is unclear and somewhat foggy. You feel stuck in your setbacks and unable to move forward freely.

- Worse = 0
- Exactly = 1
- Better = 2

Messy

Even though some things are looking up, overall life is still messy. You have some direction, but you spend so much time in the mess you feel it's keeping you from the magic and from making real progress physically, spiritually, mentally, financially, and relationally. You need some help.

- Worse = 3
- Exactly = 4
- Better = 5

Mundane

Right now things are comfortable. So far you've been able to handle most of what life has thrown at you. Things are fairly organized and nothing in your life is falling apart. You have steady relationships with little to no drama. You've developed good habits that bring order to your life, but you still feel stuck in regular mode.

- Worse = 6
- Exactly = 7
- Better = 8

Magical

It's official: you've cracked the code on life. You have not only mastered personal self-discipline and healthy relationships, you are now living in the bonus round! Even though you experience miracles everywhere you go, you know you are still a work in progress and are eager to grow more.

- Worse = 9
- Exactly = 10
- Better = 11

2. How much "magic" do you experience regularly?

Madness

It's been a long time since something magical has happened in you. If you're being honest, you feel overwhelmed with life. There is very little fun and a lot of stress.

- Worse = 0
- Exactly = 1
- Better = 2

Messy

You have experienced a few magical moments in your life, but you feel so preoccupied with the messiness of life you never feel like you have the time to do something new or go somewhere different.

- Worse = 3
- Exactly = 4
- Better = 5

Mundane

Life has been good overall, but there is very little variety. You mostly work, spend time at home, and eat at the same spots. Things are okay, but there is not much that is new in your life.

- Worse = 6
- Exactly = 7
- Better = 8

Magical

Life is not only good, but magical moments happen all the time. You always meet new people you weren't expecting and often travel to places you are interested in visiting. You have deeply spiritual experiences that make you feel connected to others, the world, and God.

- Worse = 9
- Exactly = 10
- Better = 11

3. How do you feel about your future?

Madness

You have no idea about the future. Honestly, you are barely able to handle today, let alone think about tomorrow. You live day to day, hoping for the best.

- Worse = 0
- Exactly = 1
- Better = 2

Messy

You know there is a purpose to your life, but you're struggling to make progress or have a clear sense of direction. Some of your efforts are working, but things are not moving as quickly as you'd like them to move.

- Worse = 3
- Exactly = 4
- Better = 5

Mundane

You have a clear direction in life and make regular progress toward your goals. That said, you also feel your future is a little too predictable and safe. You often find yourself wondering if there is more to life.

- Worse = 6
- Exactly = 7
- Better = 8

Magical

You are very excited about your future. You know exactly what your dreams are, and you work toward them every day and make daily progress. You are also excited about future opportunities that could lead to new projects with new people!

- Worse = 9
- Exactly = 10
- Better = 11

4. *How close are you to reaching your dreams?*

Madness

Your dreams feel a long way off—so far away that sometimes you doubt yourself. You are not moving toward your dreams, and you don't totally know how to begin working toward them.

- Worse = 0
- Exactly = 1
- Better = 2

Messy

You know what your dreams are and work toward them when you can. Honestly, that's not very often. Life keeps you so busy you struggle to find the time to work toward your goals.

- Worse = 3
- Exactly = 4
- Better = 5

Mundane

You know what you're supposed to want and regularly work toward your goals. You are making progress, but you have lost the passion you once had.

- Worse = 6
- Exactly = 7
- Better = 8

Magical

You are laser-focused on your dream. Every day you make progress and get more excited about what you're working toward, and you know why you're working toward it. Your dreams and efforts are not only incredibly meaningful to you, they inspire you to be better and strive further.

- Worse = 9
- Exactly = 10
- Better = 11

5. How much quality time do you spend with your family/kids?

Madness

You feel frustrated all the time. You don't know how to balance your personal life, work life, and family life. Your personal frustrations are affecting your family and kids. Your frustrations with your family and kids are affecting your personal and work life.

- Worse = 0
- Exactly = 1
- Better = 2

Messy

Life is messy. Your personal time is often also your family time. When you come from work frustrated you have a hard time not expressing your frustrations to your family. You need to decompress.

- Worse = 3
- Exactly = 4
- Better = 5

Mundane

Life is fairly balanced. You follow a proper schedule, which allows you to regularly schedule family time and time for yourself. That said, when you do spend time together as a family, it's spent at home. You rarely go out by yourself, with friends, or with your family and kids.

- Worse = 6
- Exactly = 7
- Better = 8

Magical

Your family is the center of your life. You have lots of fun being with one another and regularly go out and enjoy life together. You also have regular personal time by yourself, with friends, and working on your hobbies.

- Worse = 9
- Exactly = 10
- Better = 11

6. How content are you with your love life?

Madness

Your romantic life has been nonexistent for a long time. You often feel alone or lacking care, intimacy, or affection. You desire true partnership and are open to forms of romantic connection.

- Worse = 0
- Exactly = 1
- Better = 2

Messy

You experience some level of romantic connection, but it's not consistent. There is some level of intimacy and affection, but life often gets in the way, leaving you wanting more.

- Worse = 3
- Exactly = 4
- Better = 5

Mundane

You experience regular romantic connections that are meaningful. But they leave you not as fulfilled as you would like to be.

- Worse = 6
- Exactly = 7
- Better = 8

Magical

You not only experience regular meaningful romantic connections that leave you feeling extremely fulfilled, you also experience meaningful forms of intimacy and affection.

- Worse = 9
- Exactly = 10
- Better = 11

7. Do you have friends who are there for you?

Madness

You don't really have any close friends. You know people at work or from the past, but no one you could call in the middle of the night to help you out of a jam. With the friends you do have, you bond over unhealthy vices and habits.

- Worse = 0
- Exactly = 1
- Better = 2

Messy

You have one or two close friends, but they are semi-toxic relationships. Instead of them building you up, you often feel torn down and beat up after you're with them.

- Worse = 3
- Exactly = 4
- Better = 5

Mundane

You have some close friends and you get along well. You bond over common interests and past experiences. That said, you can only go so deep with them or share so much. You feel like they don't totally get you, even though you also know they love you.

- Worse = 6
- Exactly = 7
- Better = 8

Magical

You have a solid friendship group around you. You not only bond over common interests and experiences but also share the same desires. You make each other stronger. You support each other. You are better because of them. You don't know where you'd be without your most cherished friendships.

- Worse = 9
- Exactly = 10
- Better = 11

8. *What is the trajectory of your career?*

Madness

Your career has stalled. You have a job you don't like with people you can't trust. The work environment is toxic and the pay is lousy. You don't see a future working there and are unsure about working in this industry in general.

- Worse = 0
- Exactly = 1
- Better = 2

Messy

You don't like your job, but you also don't hate it. Your primary motivations for doing it are the money and security. The work culture isn't great but not bad enough for you to leave.

- Worse = 3
- Exactly = 4
- Better = 5

Mundane

Your career is doing well. You work at a good company and have a position that comes with some perks and pays well. You are reasonably happy but also feel unfulfilled. The work has become repetitive and boring. Change would be nice, but you're happy enough to stay.

- Worse = 6
- Exactly = 7
- Better = 8

Magical

You not only have a great career, you are also living your calling. Your pay is high, your coworkers are great, and you feel like you're making a real difference and creating lots of value.

- Worse = 9
- Exactly = 10
- Better = 11

9. What is your personal financial situation like?

Madness

You are in debt. You don't have a long-term personal financial plan or a budget. You avoid opening the mail in fear of finding bills or looking at the status of your bank account. You experience constant financial stress and don't have a full financial picture of your life.

- Worse = 0
- Exactly = 1
- Better = 2

Messy

You created a financial plan and a budget but don't follow it or check it often. You have reliable income but tend to spend first and ask questions later. You have some credit card debt but are making payments—usually the minimum. You have some financial stress but try not to think about it.

- Worse = 3
- Exactly = 4
- Better = 5

Mundane

You have a personal financial plan and are living within your means. You do save some money regularly but still have overhead that makes you wish you were making more.

- Worse = 6
- Exactly = 7
- Better = 8

Magical

You're not only living within your means, you have also let go of the things you can't afford. You've discovered personal financial planning, regular saving, and a modest overhead not only mean less stress and more security but also freedom!

- Worse = 9
- Exactly = 10
- Better = 11

10. How would you describe your self-care?

Madness

Self-care isn't a priority. You take no time for yourself and don't have a daily routine. You eat what you want and sleep when you want. You're not very physically active outside of walking to your car, work, and back home.

- Worse = 0
- Exactly = 1
- Better = 2

Messy

Self-care is a great idea. You make an effort at a daily routine, but you don't always follow it. You have tried dieting and exercise but have a hard time sticking to it. You've bought grooming products but don't use them regularly. You start self-improvement books but never seem to finish them.

- Worse = 3
- Exactly = 4
- Better = 5

Mundane

You have a self-care routine. For the most part, it works well. You practice good habits in health and wellness regularly and can see the results. Even so, you feel you've physically, mentally, or spiritually plateaued and find yourself wishing for more.

- Worse = 6
- Exactly = 7
- Better = 8

Magical

Self-care is not only a priority, it's become a gateway for a bigger, better, and more meaningful life. Health and wellness habits have become a lifestyle that actively and continually transform you.

- Worse = 9
- Exactly = 10
- Better = 11

APPENDIX 3

Miracle Mentality Workbook

Primary Worksheets:
1. *Magic* in the Madness
2. *Magic* in the Messy
3. *Magic* in the Mundane

Topical Worksheets:
1. Parenting
2. Love Relationships
3. Friendships
4. Work/Career
5. Money
6. Health

Magic in the Madness

The first step to overcoming the madness is to learn the power of feeding your faith and starving your doubts. You do that by *avoiding* things that drain you and *adding* activities that fuel you.

What fuels you? List activities that energize you:
Physically (e.g., Work out regularly)

_____

_____

_____

Mentally (e.g., Read a good nonfiction book)

_____

_____

_____

Spiritually (e.g., Follow a daily devotional)

_____

_____

_____

Financially (e.g., Create and review my budget)

_____

_____

_____

Relationally (e.g., Take my girlfriend out on one date a week)

_____

_____

_____

Socially (e.g., Go to the movies with my friends)

_____

_____

_____

Add Uplifting Activities

Write down two activities you'll commit to adding to your lifestyle in the next two weeks.

Activity Goal #1
Example: Reading a daily devotional

_____

Activity Goal #2
Example: Working out regularly

_____

Eliminate Draining Activities

Write down two activities that drain your energy that you can remove from your life in the next two weeks.

Draining Activity #1
Example: Sleeping in late

_____

_____

Draining Activity #2
Example: Choosing to argue with my girlfriend

_____

_____

Magic in the Messy

Before you can achieve uncommon results, you have to start living an uncommon life. That begins with taking inventory of your problem areas and developing strategies to grow in those areas.

Taking Inventory

List the areas of your life that you struggle the most with. Is it friendships? Romantic relationships? Finances? List your area and explain how you're struggling with it.

Area and Problem

Examples:

Romantic: I find myself constantly fighting with my girlfriend.
Career: I am struggling to grow my business.
Health: I feel sluggish and out of breath.
Friendship: My friend Hannah is still mad at me after I forgot her birthday.

Area

_____

Problem

_____

Area

_____

Problem

_____

Area

_____

Problem

_____

Area

_____

Problem

_____

Action Step

Sometimes the best way to address a problem area is to take the first step toward dealing with it. Below, list one action step you can take to begin to fix the problem.

Area and Action Step

Examples:

Romantic: Buy and read the book The Five Love Languages.

Career: Hire a business coach to whip me into shape.

Health: Sign up for a gym membership and schedule workout sessions during lunch.

Friendship: Call Hannah and apologize. Make it right.

Area

_____

Action Step

_____

Area

_____

Action Step

_____

Area

_____

Action Step

_____

Area

_____

Action Step

_____

Magic in the Mundane

The best way to find the magic of life is to set the conditions for something magical to happen. You set those conditions through *education*, *conversation*, and *observation*.

Education

List three topics, activities, or people you've always wanted to learn about.

Examples:

1. *Martin Luther King Jr.*
2. *How did the running of the bulls get started in Spain?*
3. *I've always wanted to learn how to ride a horse.*

1.

2.

3.

Conversation

List three topics, activities, or people you've always wanted to talk about or to.

Examples:

1. *Lewis Howes—I've always wanted to ask him how he recovered from his sports injury.*
2. *My Uncle Louis—What was it like to fight in the Korean War?*
3. *I'm really into film history. There's a Stanley Kubrick exhibit at the MOCA I want to see.*

1.

2.

3.

Observation

List three places or events you've always wanted to visit or watch and why.

Examples:

1. *Iceland—I've always wanted to see the glaciers!*
2. *An eclipse! My childhood wish was to study the stars.*
3. *Watch the movie* Pulp Fiction. *It was big in high school. Heard good things!*

1.

2.

3.

Parenting: Personal Mindset Assessment

Parenting Score Review

How much quality time do you spend with your family/kids?

Madness

You feel frustrated all the time. You don't know how to balance your personal life, work life, and family life. Your personal frustrations are affecting your family and kids. Your frustrations with your family and kids are affecting your personal and work life.

- Worse = 0
- Exactly = 1
- Better = 2

Messy

Life is messy. Your personal time is often also your family time. When you come home from work frustrated you have a hard time not expressing your frustrations to your family. You need to decompress.

- Worse = 3
- Exactly = 4
- Better = 5

Mundane

Life is fairly balanced. You follow a proper schedule, which allows you to regularly schedule family time and time for yourself. That said, when you do spend time together as a family, it's spent at home. You rarely go out by yourself, with friends, or with your family and kids.

- Worse = 6
- Exactly = 7
- Better = 8

Magical

Your family is the center of your life. You have lots of fun being with one another and regularly go out and enjoy life together. You also have regular personal time by yourself, with friends, and working on your hobbies.

- Worse = 9
- Exactly = 10
- Better = 11

YOUR SCORE: _____ (0–11)

YOUR STATE: _____ (MADNESS | MESSY | MUNDANE | MAGICAL)

Magic in Parenting

The best way to move from the mundane to the magical in parenting is to lower personal frustration and increase your parenting *patience*, *energy*, and *creativity*. Increase your capacity by choosing one activity to do with yourself, with your romantic partner or a friend, and with your children in each of these three key areas.

Increase Patience

Examples:

1. *By Yourself: Go to a yoga class.*
2. *With Partner or Friend: Go ice skating in Central Park.*
3. *With Kid(s): Make hot chocolate together and watch a classic movie.*

1. By Yourself

_____

2. With Partner or Friend

_____

3. With Kid(s)

_____

Increase Energy

Examples:

1. *By Yourself: Go for a brisk jog while listening to my favorite music.*
2. *With Partner or Friend: Go on a romantic date or for drinks with friends at a trendy restaurant or bar.*
3. *With Kid(s): Take them to play laser tag.*

1. By Yourself

_____

2. With Partner or Friend

_____

3. With Kid(s)

_____

Increase Creativity

Examples:

1. *By Yourself: Take music or singing lessons.*
2. *With Partner or Friend: Attend a cooking class.*
3. *With Kid(s): Go to the beach and build a sand castle.*

1. By Yourself

_____

2. With Partner or Friend

_____

3. With Kid(s)

_____

Love Relationships: Personal Mindset Assessment

Love Relationship Score Review
How content are you with your love life?

Madness

Your romantic life has been nonexistent for a long time. You often feel alone or lacking care, intimacy, or affection. You desire true partnership and are open to forms of romantic connection.

- Worse = 0
- Exactly = 1
- Better = 2

Messy

You experience some level of romantic connection, but it's not consistent. There is some level of intimacy and affection, but life often gets in the way, leaving you wanting more.

- Worse = 3
- Exactly = 4
- Better = 5

Mundane

You experience regular romantic connections that are meaningful. But they leave you not as fulfilled as you would like to be.

- Worse = 6
- Exactly = 7
- Better = 8

Magical

You not only experience regular meaningful romantic connections that leave you feeling extremely fulfilled, you also experience meaningful forms of intimacy and affection.

- Worse = 9
- Exactly = 10
- Better = 11

YOUR SCORE: _____ (0–11)
YOUR STATE: _____ (MADNESS | MESSY | MUNDANE | MAGICAL)

Magic in Love Relationships

The cornerstone for long-term success in love relationships begins with *connection* and *cultivation*. That means keeping up the things that cultivated your initial connection and love.

Take Your Partner on a Date

Examples:

- *Take my partner to a dinner and a movie.*
- *Cook a romantic dinner at home.*
- *Spend the weekend in the wine country.*
- *Go get a couples' massage.*

Date Ideas:

_____

_____

_____

_____

_____

_____

Have a Meaningful Conversation

Examples:

- *Discuss shared future goals.*
- *Spend time connecting over common interests.*
- *Talk about how you first met and fell in love.*
- *Share dream vacation ideas.*

Topics to Discuss:

_____

_____

_____

_____

Perform Acts of Love

Examples:

- *Do the dishes for them after a long day at work.*
- *Buy them flowers or bring them lunch at work.*
- *Write them a sweet card or note of encouragement.*
- *Take the kids to Disneyland while your partner enjoys a day at the spa.*

Nice Things You Could Do for Your Partner:

_____

_____

_____

_____

Friendships: Personal Mindset Assessment

Friendships Score Review
Do you have friends who are there for you?

Madness

You don't really have any close friends. You know people at work or from the past, but no one you could call in the middle of the night to help you out of a jam. With the friends you do have, you bond over unhealthy vices and habits.

- Worse = 0
- Exactly = 1
- Better = 2

Messy

You have one or two close friends, but they are semi-toxic relationships. Instead of them building you up, you often feel torn down and beat up after you're with them.

- Worse = 3
- Exactly = 4
- Better = 5

Mundane

You have some close friends and you get along well. You bond over common interests and past experiences. That said, you can only go so deep with them or share so much. You feel like they don't totally get you, even though you also know they love you.

- Worse = 6
- Exactly = 7
- Better = 8

Magical

You have a solid friendship group around you. You not only bond over common interests and experiences but also share the same desires. You make each other stronger. You support each other. You are better because of them. You don't know where you'd be without your most cherished friendships.

- Worse = 9
- Exactly = 10
- Better = 11

YOUR SCORE: _____ (0–11)
YOUR STATE: _____ (MADNESS | MESSY | MUNDANE | MAGICAL)

Magic in Friendship

An Exercise to Do with a Friend: Power of Partnership
Name of friend you're partnering with:_____
Example: Tom Anderson

An Exercise in Listening
Ask them to explain what they want their life to look like in the next three to five years. Write it down:
Example:
Tom's dream is to become a musician. He wants to make all of his money as a working artist and finally leave his job as a waiter. He also wants to develop as an actor, so he wants to sign up for an acting class.

Tom also wants to get a dog. A German shepherd. He's just been waiting to finally make the leap.

It's been over a year since Tom broke up with his longtime girl-friend. He is finally ready to meet new people and go on dates. He wants a relationship. This is very big for him! Go, Tom!

_____

_____

_____

Areas

If you had to name the three main areas that are the focus of their goals, what would they be?

Examples:

1. *Music*
2. *Finances*
3. *Romantic Relationships*

1.

2.

3.

Support

Write down three ways you can support them in reaching their goals.

Examples:

1. *I can make sure to go to Tom's local shows to support him!*
2. *When Tom wants to go out and meet new people, I can be his wingman and encourage him!*

3. *When Tom gets his dog and needs someone to house-sit while he's away touring, I can help!*

1.

2.

3.

Work/Career: Personal Mindset Assessment

Work/Career Score Review
What is the trajectory of your career?

Madness

Your career has stalled. You have a job you don't like with people you can't trust. The work environment is toxic and the pay is lousy. You don't see a future working there and are unsure about working in this industry in general.

- Worse = 0
- Exactly = 1
- Better = 2

Messy

You don't like your job, but you also don't hate it. Your primary motivations for doing it are the money and security. The work culture isn't great but not bad enough for you to leave.

- Worse = 3
- Exactly = 4
- Better = 5

Mundane

Your career is doing well. You work at a good company and have a position that comes with some perks and pays well. You are reasonably happy but also feel unfulfilled. The work has become repetitive and boring. Change would be nice, but you're happy enough to stay.

- Worse = 6
- Exactly = 7
- Better = 8

Magical

You're not only living within your means, you also have let go of the things you can't afford. You have found that personal financial planning, disciplined savings, and a modest overhead not only mean less stress and more security, but also freedom!

- Worse = 9
- Exactly = 10
- Better = 11

YOUR SCORE: _____ (0–11)

YOUR STATE: _____ (MADNESS | MESSY | MUNDANE | MAGICAL)

Magic in Work/Career

Proverbs 28:19 says, "Those who work their land will have abundant food" (NIV). If you want to experience abundance in your career, start by working hard and sowing good seeds!

Prosper Where You're Planted

Build your career opportunities by working hard and developing a good reputation. Create a vision for your future by describing what you would want your coworkers or boss to say about you at a performance review.

Example:

I want them to say that I am excellent at my job. That I always put my best foot toward. That I am reliable, dependable, and always willing to help out. I also want them to say that I am positive and encouraging. That I am a fun person to work with and I lift up the team when I am there.

If there is a promotion, I want them to think of me. That I would be up for any challenge, that I can take criticism well, be responsible, and own my failures and successes.

_____

_____

_____

_____

Work Your Land

Some jobs don't last forever. That said, use your current opportunity to set you up for long-term success. Write down three skills this job has taught you that you could take into future opportunities.

Example:

1. *I'm a master at Photoshop.*
2. *I can type sixty words a minute.*
3. *I can lead a team.*

1.

2.

3.

Sow Good Seeds

Who are three people at your work or job you can support, encourage, or help? And what can you do to bless them over the next month?

Example:

1. *My boss, Briana: Figure out what she needs before she asks.*
2. *Teammate Jon: Encourage him. It's been a hard sales month.*
3. *Janitor Steve: Leave him a thank-you note for all his hard work.*

Name #1

_____

Way I Can Help Them

_____

Name #2

_____

Way I Can Help Them

_____

Name #3

_____

Way I Can Help Them

_____

Money: Personal Mindset Assessment

Money Score Review
What is your personal financial situation like?

Madness

You are in debt. You don't have a long-term personal financial plan or a budget. You avoid opening the mail in fear of finding bills or looking at the status of your bank account. You experience constant financial stress and don't have a full financial picture of your life.

- Worse = 0
- Exactly = 1
- Better = 2

Messy

You created a financial plan and a budget but don't follow it or check it often. You have reliable income but tend to spend first and ask questions later. You have some credit card debt but are making payments—usually the minimum. You have some financial stress but try not to think about it.

- Worse = 3
- Exactly = 4
- Better = 5

Mundane

You have a personal financial plan and are living within your means. You do save some money regularly but still have overhead that makes you wish you were making more.

- Worse = 6
- Exactly = 7
- Better = 8

Magical

You're not only living within your means, you have also let go of the things you can't afford. You've discovered personal financial planning, regular saving, and a modest overhead not only mean less stress and more security but also freedom!

- Worse = 9
- Exactly = 10
- Better = 11

YOUR SCORE: _____ (0–11)
YOUR STATE: _____ (MADNESS | MESSY | MUNDANE | MAGICAL)

Magic in Money

What Matters

The first step to magical finances is to identify what matters most in your life. Is your luxury car really more important than meaningful relationships, joy, or peace? Describe three of the most important non-material things in your life.

Example:

1. *Family*
2. *Security*
3. *Making a difference*

1.

2.

3.

Eliminate

Step two is to declutter your financial life. That happens when you eliminate financial waste. Write a list of three to five things you pay for right now that you could eliminate in the next thirty days.

Examples:

Things You Don't Need

- *HBO, Showtime, Hulu, and cable (I don't need all of those!)*
- *Monthly spa membership*
- *Designer jeans*
- *Takeout every night*

Things You Don't Need

_____

_____

_____

_____

_____

Downsize

Step three is to downsize. Do you really need the big house with empty bedrooms when something more modest will do? List three things you could downsize within the next year.

Example:
Current Asset ? and Downsized Version

1. *Luxury car ? Reliable car*
2. *Boat ? I can rent a boat.*
3. *Large house ? Spacious apartment in the city*

Current Asset ? and Downsized Version

1.

2.

3.

Health: Personal Mindset Assessment

Health Score Review
How would you describe your self-care?

Madness

Self-care isn't a priority. You take no time for yourself and don't have a daily routine. You eat what you want and sleep when you want. You're not very physically active outside of walking to your car, work, and back home.

- Worse = 0
- Exactly = 1
- Better = 2

Messy

Self-care is a great idea. You make an effort at a daily routine, but you don't always follow it. You have tried dieting and exercise but have a hard time sticking to it. You've bought grooming products but don't use them regularly. You start self-improvement books but never seem to finish them.

- Worse = 3
- Exactly = 4
- Better = 5

Mundane

You have a self-care routine. For the most part, it works well. You practice good habits in health and wellness regularly and can see the results. Even so, you feel you've physically, mentally, or spiritually plateaued and find yourself wishing for more.

- Worse = 6
- Exactly = 7
- Better = 8

Magical

Self-care is not only a priority, it's become a gateway for a bigger, better, and more meaningful life. Health and wellness habits have become a lifestyle that actively and continuously transforms your life.

- Worse = 9
- Exactly = 10
- Better = 11

YOUR SCORE: _____ (0–11)

YOUR STATE: _____ (MADNESS | MESSY | MUNDANE | MAGICAL)

Magic in Health

Vision

What does being healthy look like to you? Travel into the future two to three years from now. If you had all the time, money, and help you needed, what would your life look like at peak self-care?

Example:

I'd like to be an active man who still has a lot of energy and feels good in his body. I'd like to be working out at least three mornings a week and at my ideal weight and still be able to fit in the same size shirts and pants as I did in my thirties and forties. I want a regular morning self-care routine that prepares me for the day wherever I am (even when traveling). I want to feel strong and capable physically but also mentally. Even though I am busy I want to be reading at least one book a week and still learning new things!

_____

_____

_____

_____

_____

Revelation

If you had to describe your future self in three words, what would they be?

Example:

1. *Strong*
2. *Slim*
3. *Clean cut*

1.

2.

3.

Action

Having great self-care means establishing great self-care habits. What are three simple habits you can begin this week that will move you closer to your health vision for your life?

Example:

1. *I can begin my day by drinking a green smoothie for breakfast that includes all my daily vitamins.*
2. *I can schedule a walk with my son on Tuesdays and Thursdays after work at the local park.*
3. *I will spend time reading a devotional and journaling thirty minutes each morning before I check my phone, emails, or social media.*

1.

2.

3.

Acknowledgments

Maya Angelou once said, "Try and be a rainbow in someone's cloud."

As I was writing *The Miracle Mentality*, I encountered mostly sunshine, but I still came across gloomy days when I needed a rainbow. Lucky for me, a rainbow always seemed to appear whenever I needed it. The following individuals all served as lovely rainbows—miracles, if you will—in my life.

Thank you, Dianne Hudson, the former executive producer of the Oprah Winfrey Show, for believing in me enough to suggest to her dear friend that I would be a good guest for her *SuperSoul Sunday* show. I must have done okay, because Ms. Winfrey called on me for other projects; she has now become a dear friend. I am not the first to say Oprah Winfrey helped change my life.

To Quincy Jones, Berry Gordy, Smokey Robinson, Leon Isaac Kennedy, and Suzanne de Passe, some of my mentors in life and in entertainment, thank you for saying I was next. And thank you, Quincy, for labeling me "the voice of encouragement for this generation."

To Nick Chiles, an amazing man and a great writer and teacher. You stretched me, challenged me, helped me become a much better storyteller, pushed me to dig deeper and bring out sides of my writing I didn't even know were there. It is an honor to call you my friend.

This book could not have been possible without the guidance of Spencer Proffer. His wisdom helped guide me to the right team. He assisted me on a weekly basis to develop a much clearer idea of what the Miracle Mentality really is and encouraged me to believe I was equipped to bring forth the message. His wife, Judy Proffer, has a gift with words that truly jump off the page. She helped sharpen my writing skills with her advice and beautiful soul.

Thank you also to my amazing agents, Jeff Silberman and Scott Hoffman, truly a dream team. I can see why you guys are among the best in the business. And an extra thank you to Jeff for our deep conversations about life, for bringing out the best in me, for becoming my friend and not just my agent, and for being one of my favorite people—one who takes the time to make others feel warm and welcomed.

A deep, heartfelt thank you to everyone at Harper Horizon, who served as midwives to help bring this book to life. Andrea Fleck-Nisbet, my publisher, who believed in my message and showed me so much thoughtfulness, sharing my vision from day one. Amanda Bauch, my editor, whose patience and deft touch helped make the words sing. John Andrade, Harper Horizon's marketing director, for your passion, your tireless efforts, and for realizing the world needs a book like this. Elizabeth Much, our publicist, for opening doors and new possibilities. You all have been an absolute joy to work with.

And a special thank you to my team—my friend and fabulous attorney, Keith Berglund; Joseph Mendoza, my right-hand man, who helps me beautifully manifest my projects; Stefan Junaeus, a brilliant guy who helped craft the Miracle Mindset Workbook and Assessment that became such an important part of this book.

This book has my name on it, but you have all been a big part of it, and of me.

Notes

Chapter 2: Toiling in the Mundane, the Messy, and the Mad

1. Neel Burton, "Our Hierarchy of Needs," *Psychology Today*, May 23, 2012 (revised May 4, 2020), https://www.psychologytoday.com/us/blog/hide-and-seek/201205/our-hierarchy-needs.

Chapter 4: Parenting

1. D. Saxbe and R. L. Repetti, "For Better or Worse? Coregulation of Couples' Cortisol Levels and Mood States," *Journal of Personal Social Psychology* 98, no. 1 (January 2010): 92–103, doi: 10.1037/a0016959.
2. "Tidier Homes, Fitter Bodies?," Indiana University Newsroom, accessed July 3, 2020, https://newsinfo.iu.edu/web/page/normal/14627.html.
3. Shilpa Ravinder et al., "Excessive Sensory Stimulation During Development Alters Neural Plasticity and Vulnerability to Cocaine in Mice," *eNeuro* 3, no. 4 (July–August 2016), doi: 10.1523/ENEURO.0199-16.2016.
4. Quincy Jones, *Q: The Autobiography of Quincy Jones* (New York: Random House, 2001), 5.
5. Jones, *Q*, 14.

Chapter 5: Love Relationships

1. Deborah Carr et al., "Happy Marriage, Happy Life? Marital Quality and Subjective Well-Being in Later Life," *Journal of Marriage and Family* 75, no. 5 (October 2014): 930–48, doi: 10.1111/jomf.12133.
2. J. K. Kiecolt-Glaser et al., "Marital Distress, Depression, and a Leaky Gut: Translocation of Bacterial Endotoxin as a Pathway to Inflammation," *Psychoneuroendocrinology* 98 (December 2018): 52–60, doi: 10.1016/j.psyneuen.2018.08.007.
3. Timothy W. Smith and Brian R. W. Baucom, "Intimate Relationships, Individual Adjustment, and Coronary Heart Disease: Implications of Overlapping Associations in Psychosocial Risk," *American Psychologist* 72, no. 6 (September 2017): 578–89, doi: 10.1037/amp0000123.
4. *Urban Mobility Report: 2019*, Texas A&M Transportation Institute, accessed July 3, 2020, https://mobility.tamu.edu/umr/congestion-data/.
5. George L. Kelling and James Q. Wilson, "Broken Windows: The Police and Neighborhood Safety," *Atlantic*, March 1982, https://www.theatlantic.com/magazine/archive/1982/03/broken-windows/304465/.

Chapter 6: Friendships

1. Noah C, "Diddy & Kevin Hart Make Motivational Toasts at Roc Nation Brunch," *Hot New Hip Hop*, January 26, 2020, https://www.hotnewhiphop.com/diddy-and-kevin-hart-make-motivational-toasts-at-roc-nation-brunch-news.101974.html.

Chapter 7: Work/Career

1. "4 Lessons in Employee Empowerment, Courtesy of Chick-fil-A," Customer Service Profiles, accessed July 3, 2020, https://www.csp.com/chick-fil-a/#.Xv9y7yhKg2x.
2. *Big*, directed by Penny Marshall (Los Angeles: Twentieth Century Fox, 1988).
3. Rochel Chein, "What Is the Meaning of the Name 'Jew'?," accessed July 3, 2020, https://www.chabad.org/library/article_cdo/aid/640221/jewish/What-is-the-Meaning-of-the-Name-Jew.htm.

4. "Time Flies: U.S. Adults Now Spend Nearly Half a Day Interacting with Media," The Nielsen Company, July 31, 2018, https://www.nielsen.com/us/en/insights/article/2018/time-flies-us-adults-now-spend-nearly-half-a-day-interacting-with-media/.

Chapter 9: Health

1. "The Power of the Placebo Effect," Harvard Men's Health Watch, updated August 9, 2019, https://www.health.harvard.edu/mental-health/the-power-of-the-placebo-effect.

2. Barna Group, "Most Americans Believe in Supernatural Healing," September 29, 2016, https://www.barna.com/research/americans-believe-supernatural-healing/.

3. Craig M. Hales et al., "Prevalence of Obesity and Severe Obesity Among Adults: United States, 2017–2018," *NCHS Data Brief*, no. 360 (February 2020): 1–8, https://www.cdc.gov/nchs/products/databriefs/db360.htm.

4. "U.S. Health Care Spending Highest Among Developed Countries," Johns Hopkins Bloomberg School of Public Health, January 7, 2019, https://www.jhsph.edu/news/news-releases/2019/us-health-care-spending-highest-among-developed-countries.html.

5. Lee J. Miller and Wei Lu, "These Are the World's Healthiest Nations," Bloomberg, February 24, 2019, https://www.bloomberg.com/news/articles/2019-02-24/spain-tops-italy-as-world-s-healthiest-nation-while-u-s-slips.

6. Al Sharpton, *The Rejected Stone: Al Sharpton and the Path to American Leadership* (New York: Cash Money Content, 2013), p. 211–12.

7. Sharpton, *Rejected Stone*, 207.

About the Authors

Tim Storey is an acclaimed author, speaker, and life coach, known for inspiring and motivating people of all walks of life, from entertainment executives, celebrities, and athletes to adults and children in the most deprived neighborhoods in the country. Tim has traveled to seventy-five countries and spoken to millions of people. He often meets privately to counsel high-profile leaders in various industries.

Along with a rigorous speaking calendar and private life-coaching sessions, Tim regularly appears on nationally syndicated radio and television shows and has hosted an exclusive Saturday morning series on SiriusXM Radio. Recently, Tim was interviewed for a full-hour segment of Oprah Winfrey's OWN *SuperSoul Sunday*. Since then, he has been a speaker for SuperSoul Sessions LIVE from UCLA and was a guest speaker at the ultra-exclusive PTTOW! (Plan to Take on the World) Summit in Palos Verdes, California.

Tim also leads The Congregation Church in Placentia, California, which meets weekly and provides spiritual insight and direction for people of diverse ages, backgrounds, and needs.

About the Authors

Nick Chiles is a Pulitzer Prize–winning journalist and the author or coauthor of nineteen books, including three *New York Times* bestsellers. He teaches journalism at the University of Georgia.